Programs for Special Occasions

by
Matilda Nordtvedt
and
Pearl Steinkuehler

MOODY PRESS
CHICAGO

© 1984 by
THE MOODY BIBLE INSTITUTE
OF CHICAGO

All rights reserved. No part of this book may be reproduced in any
form without permission in writing from the publisher, except in the
case of brief quotations embodied in critical articles or reviews.

All Scripture quotations in this book, unless otherwise noted, are
from the *New American Standard Bible*, © 1960, 1962, 1963, 1968,
1971, 1972, 1973, 1975, and 1977 by The Lockman Foundation, and
are used by permission.

The use of selected references from various versions of the Bible in
this publication does not necessarily imply publisher endorsement
of the versions in their entirety.

ISBN 0-8024-1218-1

1 2 3 4 5 6 7 Printing/B+/Year 89 88 87 86 85 84

Printed in the United States of America

Contents

Introduction

"Where can I find a poem to read at my folks' wedding anniversary?"

"We're getting a new pastor, and I'm in charge of the welcome service. What do I do?"

"It would be nice to honor our graduates, but where would we find ideas for a program?"

"Our church is having an anniversary celebration. I need to come up with something interesting."

"What do you do at a church dedication anyway?"

If you have asked those questions at one time or another, this book will provide some answers for you. It has been written to help you with your celebrations. You will find program ideas, poems that fit the occasion, and suggestions for decorations.

Happy celebrating!

Introduction

"When ... I like a poem to read at my folks' wedding anniversary."

"We're having a new pastor and I'm in charge of the social. What shall I do?"

"It would be nice to honor our graduates, but where would we find time for a program?"

"Our church is having an anniversary celebration and I need to come up with something interesting."

"When do you want this special occasion anyway?"

If you have asked those questions at one time or another, this book will provide some answers for you. It has been written to help you with your celebrations. You will find here many ideas, poems that fit the occasion and suggestions for programs.

Happy celebrating!

1
Wedding Anniversary

> Grow old along with me
> The best is yet to be,
> The last of life, for which the first was made:
> Our times are in his hand . . .
>
> —Robert Browning

A wedding anniversary is a celebration of: the aging process, the discovery that life together gets better day by day, and the affirmation that the future is in God's hands.

Webster defines this event as "returning annually; the annual recurrence of a date marking a notable event." An anniversary is an appropriate time to commemorate the attainment of success in Christian marriage. It is a romantic time, a private time, a public time, a serious time, a joyous time, a time to praise the Lord.

Why have anniversary celebrations? A marriage that has survived the pressures of today's world is something to celebrate! A Christ-honoring celebration of a happy couple can do at least three things.

It can remind all present of God's stated plan for marriage and Jesus' interpretation of the plan. In Genesis 2:24, after He had created Eve for Adam, God said, "For this cause a man shall leave his father and his mother, and shall cleave to his wife; and they shall become one flesh." Jesus affirmed the permanence of this union in Matthew 19:6: "Consequently they are no longer two, but one flesh. What therefore God has joined together, let no man separate."

Remembering the happy days and receiving the best wishes of friends and relatives can improve the years ahead for the couple being honored.

Anniversary celebrations inspire young people and others present to determine to build a "till death do us part" marriage for themselves.

The earliest references to family celebration in English literature go back to the 1659 diary of John Evelyn where he mentions an invitation to a forty-first wedding-day feast. Samuel Pepys in his diary wrote of going home "to be merry, it being my sixth wedding night."

The custom of celebrating wedding anniversaries with particular gifts dates back to the medieval Germans. If a married couple lived to celebrate the twenty-fifth anniversary of their wedding, friends and neighbors gave the wife a silver wreath. This said, "Congratulations for good health and harmony. You must get along fairly harmoniously or you would have already worried each other into the grave by now!"

Rarely did couples then live long enough to celebrate fifty years together. Those who did were given a golden wreath of congratulations. Thus the twenty-fifth and fiftieth anniversaries came to be known as silver wedding-day and golden wedding-day respectively.[1]

Churches were involved in celebrations in 1624 as an early church record in that year refers to "sylver brydells," but those were rare since few people lived so long.

The first references to the golden wedding appears in an 1860 London newspaper. The diamond wedding anniversary was first mentioned in *Punch* in 1872, referring to any year after sixty, seventy, or seventy-five years. The symbols for other anniversaries seem to have evolved comparatively recently.

1. Robert Thorne, *Fugitive Facts* (reprint, Ann Arbor, Mich.: Gryphon Books, 1971), p. 446

In seventeenth-century England every anniversary seems to have been the occasion for a party with family and friends. In America today husbands and wives remember their special date annually with parties and friends and sometimes just the two of them.

Who Gives The Party?

Usually the couple themselves give it. By the twenty-fifth anniversary, they may have grown children who wish to make the arrangements, but it is perfectly correct for them to host the party if the young people do not or cannot. Almost invariably a fiftieth anniversary celebration is planned by the family of the couple. Often grandchildren assist in the plans and program.

Who Is Invited?

The guest list is often determined by the size of the event. If it is to be a small party, the family, members of the wedding party, and closest friends are invited. If a large gathering is planned, business acquaintances, church and club members and, in very small communities, everyone in town is welcomed.

If a reception is held, guests usually include the members of both families of the couple, the attendants and guests who came to the wedding, and other friends the couple chooses to invite.

At a dinner, the guest list will need to be smaller. Only the family members and close friends are invited usually.

When Should It Be Given?

When convenient, have the anniversary celebration on the actual date of the anniversary. If that is not possible, the date can be adjusted to the nearest suitable weekend to aid out-of-town guests.

Where Should It Be?

The usual places include the home of the couple, the home of the person planning the party, a church fellowship hall, or a meeting room of a hotel, restaurant, or club. It may be held outdoors in a garden or park if circumstances are convenient. If the couple had a garden wedding it would be fitting to celebrate an anniversary in the garden also.

What Do You Do?

Generally a brief program of music, readings, or skits is given by the children or grandchildren of the couple along with a short devotional by the pastor or other friend. This is followed by opening of gifts, cards, letters, and telegrams and the serving of refreshments.

The leading forms of celebrations are: an informal open house in the afternoon or evening, a more formal reception, a family dinner, or a combination of those.

A receiving line is usual. The couple and any members of their bridal party present stand near the entrance as they did at the wedding reception. Their children may join them. If the party is given by another member of the family, that person should head the line as hostess. Or the host couple could serve as greeters and mingle among the guests throughout the party.

If the couple being honored is elderly and tires easily, they may be seated in a central spot instead of standing in a reception line. Guests should be greeted by the hostess at the door and then move on to the honored pair to offer them their congratulations.

To give a successful anniversary celebration:

Determine the date early.

Plan well in advance with committees who will share the work load. Since some guests may come from great distances and will need to arrange time off from work, they should be notified of the date and general plans six months to a year in advance.

4

Reserve the meeting place several months in advance.

Contact persons involved. That may include the florist, the caterer, the baker, the minister, the members of the original wedding party, and close friends and family from near and far.

Advertise the activity by mouth, invitations, posters, newspaper ads, and church bulletins as the date approaches.

Decorate in keeping with the program theme.

PROGRAMS

Weave (We've) Only Just Begun

A simplified weaving could be made during the program (directions follow) while someone speaks the following words:

Speaker: God's plan for marriage is that the two will leave their former lives, cleave to one another, and become one flesh. It takes a lot of living to weave two lives into one beautiful tapestry. _____ and _____ have shown us how two lives can be meshed into one.

Let's examine these lovely lives to see what qualities have gone into their bright beginning. We've seen many of the threads they have woven into their loom of life. Some are more easily noticed than others. Some are in subtle hues.

Their commitment to each other and to the importance of marriage is obvious. Their desire to keep their home Christ-centered is prominent. Close examination indicates that they work at communication. They seek to develop understanding and honesty in their relationships with one another. Courtesy aids in the blending.

Love reigns in their home. _____ and _____ reserve time for each other so the demands of a busy life won't make them strangers who only eat and sleep under the same roof. They trust each other to work at keeping their relationship of primary importance. A sense of humor and times of fun lighten and brighten days that could become boring and commonplace. The pain and tears that are common to all have come into their lives as well. Those subtle shades too add depth to the tapestry of life.

Lives focused only upon each other would soon become stagnant. Friends have been added to the loom to bless and be blessed by their tapestry of life.

(Show the weaving visual.)

_____ and _____ would be the first to say, "We've only just begun." They have much more living to experience before the tapestry of life is completed.

On this _____ anniversary, we congratulate you on a successful beginning and commend you to the Lord as you keep on weaving.

To make the "tapestry":

On a large piece of light-weight cardboard draw 1-inch squares, 21 from left to right and 13 from top to bottom. Leave a 1-inch border at the top and left side. For ease in weaving, number the squares on the board 21 across and 13 down with pencil. Color every other lengthwise row one of the two theme colors; leave the alternating rows uncolored. Cut 7 strips of the other theme color 1 inch wide and 13 squares long. Mark 1-inch squares on these strips.

Cut from right to left on the lines between the horizontal strips leaving one inch of uncut border on the left side. You should finish with 13 horizontal strips attached at the left and with a border at the top. With a dark marker, letter the uncolored horizontal strips (one letter to a square) with the words *courtesy, honesty, communication, Christ-centered* (have the dash cover 2 squares), *commitment,* and *understanding.* Capital letters are more readable from a distance.

With another color, letter the separate vertical strips as illustrated. Tape the vertical strips on the back side of squares 2, 4, 7, 13, 15, and 20 as shown. Fold these back until you are ready to begin weaving.

After attention has been called to the horizontal words by the speaker, lay the tapestry board on a table and weave in the vertical words as the speaker talks about those qualities in the couple's life. The simplest way to weave them in is to lift horizontal row 2 and lay it over the number 2 squares of all of the vertical strips at once. Do the same with horizontal rows 4, 6, 8, 10, and 12.

Some letters on the vertical strips will be covered. Complete the vertical words by printing the covered letters in the same color as the other vertical letters.

Glue or tape the ends of the vertical pieces and the right border of the horizontal strips in place.

Display the "Weave Only Just Begun" tapestry to the guests. You may wish to present this simple object lesson to the honored couple at the close of the program. (See illustration on pp. 8-9.)

As a variation (if you wish to use an easier-to-construct illustration) chart an acrostic lettered as illustrated in the theme colors. You may wish to list other applicable things or qualities a couple needs to weave a beautiful life tapestry together.

Tapestry Acrostic:

W orship	J esus
E xpression	U nanimous
A cceptance	S elflessness
V aluing	T ogetherness
E njoyment	
	B ible
O bservant	E xcitement
N urturing	G aiety
L ove	U nderstanding
Y ielding	N eighbors

Devotional comments could be adjusted to include references to: *worship* experiences at home and church, freedom in *expression* of feelings, *acceptance* of each other as they are, *valuing* each other as the most important person in their world, and sharing the *enjoyment* of life together.

Mention that they are *observant* of each other's needs, *nurturing* in the mutual building up of one another that they might become the best they are capable of becoming, demonstrating *love* and *yielding* to the other's wishes.

7

[Do not cut past double line.]

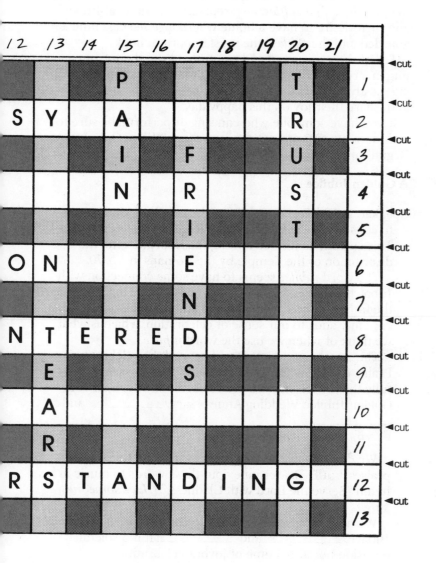

Include *Jesus* as the Lord of their home, their ability to dis-
cuss conflicts until a *unanimous* agreement can be reached,
to make sure that *selflessness* replaces "me first" attitudes,
and their desire to have a home where *togetherness* time is
guarded and the *Bible* is the most important book.

Tell of the *excitement* and *gaiety* that keep them from getting in a rut and the *understanding* that is constantly growing. Lastly, include the friends and *neighbors* who are invited
in to share their joy on this happy day.

If you have someone who can sing or perform, be sure to
include some appropriate songs such as: "We've Only Just
Begun" and "Love Is Commitment."

A Golden Jubilee

Speaker: In Old Testament times the people of God were told
to consecrate the fiftieth year. *(Read Leviticus 25:10-12a.)*
This custom continued among the Hebrews until the
destruction of the Temple by the Romans in A.D. 70.

The word *jubilee* seems to have some connection with
Jubal, the descendant of Cain who is named in Genesis as
the father of those who play the harp and the organ. Music
certainly adds to our sense of celebration, which is what
we think of when we use the word *jubilee.*

The sweet songwriter David penned the celebrative
Psalm 100 known as "The Jubilate." It expresses beauti-
fully the joy we know as we celebrate with you on your
Golden Jubilee Wedding Anniversary, _____ and

_____.

(Read Psalm 100.)

We don't know the tune David sang with these lovely
praises, but B. B. McKinney put these words to music in his
hymn "Serve the Lord with Gladness." *(Have someone
sing.)*

We have met together today to consecrate your Golden
Jubilee, _____ and _____. It is a solemn
occasion but also a time of joyous celebration.

A fiftieth anniversary in today's world of uncertainties is
becoming a bit of a rarity. Many couples give up on
marriage—some after only a few months. We rejoice with

you in your commitment to each other. Your steadfast love is an inspiration to us.

Will you share with us the secret of how you have reached this golden day?

(Allow time for their responses. Bridge their thoughts with appropriate comments in relation to their answers.)

Supplement these thoughts with the Fiftieth Anniversary poem on page 37. Close the devotional time with prayer, thanking God for the happy occasion and asking His blessings on their years to come.

Alumni of the School of Wedded Bliss

Conduct a graduation exercise for the couple you honor on their anniversary. This theme would be especially appropriate for a couple connected with an educational institution or one whose anniversary date is near graduation time.

Print a program as illustrated, folded with the bottom extending from under the top far enough to show the last line of the class motto. Use ink and paper in the wedding colors of the couple.

School Crest

Program Folder

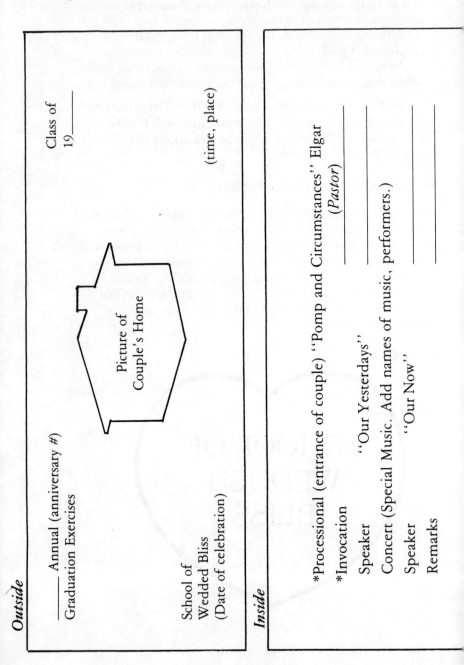

Outside

_____ Annual (anniversary #)
Graduation Exercises

Class of
19 ___

Picture of
Couple's Home

School of
Wedded Bliss
(Date of celebration)

(time, place)

Inside

*Processional (entrance of couple) "Pomp and Circumstances," Elgar

*Invocation   (*Pastor*)

Speaker   "Our Yesterdays"

Concert (Special Music. Add names of music, performers.)

Speaker   "Our Now"

Remarks

Speaker   "Our Tomorrows"

Presentation of Class, Diplomas

*Benediction

      "Wedding March" Mendelssohn

*Recessional   Reception following

*Audience stands

All our Yesterdays are summarized in our NOW,

and

ALL OUR TOMORROWS ARE OURS TO SHAPE

ALL OUR TOMORROWS ARE OURS TO SHAPE

Choose relatives or close friends to speak during the program. The first speaker can tell anecdotes from the couple's past entitled "Our Yesterdays." The second speaker should tell of present happenings entitled "Our Now." The third speaker could cover "Our Tomorrows" and encourage the couple to follow the teachings of the Scripture just read to continue to shape their future after God's plan.

Remarks should be delivered by the master of ceremonies, who also presents the class (honorees) and diplomas. He should talk about the class motto and read Psalm 37:1-9.

Present the couple a diploma as illustrated. This diploma may be a simple scroll with the following message or may be a fancy folder of leatherette and satin with fancy lettering making it a keepsake.

After greeting the honorees in a receiving line ("recessional" on program), guests should adjourn to the fellowship hall where favorite love songs of the couple could provide background music while the guests wait for the honorees to arrive.

Continue the graduation theme in the decor of the hall and serving table. Put a large poster of the school crest on the wall behind the gift table. Drape an arch of crepe paper streamers over the serving table. Top the anniversary cake with a replica of the school crest with a small bride and groom standing in front of it. Arrange small pompons and mortarboard nutcups in the couple's colors on the table. (See page 87 for mortarboard nutcup instructions.)

As a different memento, present the "graduates" an autograph hound wearing a mortarboard, and allow guests an opportunity to sign it for them.

As guests leave, give them a diploma-like scroll tied with embroidery thread in the theme colors, thanking them for being part of this happy occasion.

Love Is a Bridge

Speaker: A bridge is defined by Webster as "a structure carrying a pathway or roadway over a depression or obstacle; a time, place, or means of connection or transition."

A look at the word *bridge* reveals that it contains the word *bride* with the inclusion of a *g.* Let's imagine the *g*

14

SCHOOL OF WEDDED BLISS

town, state

_____ and _____

having completed the course of study prescribed for the

degree of

BACHELOR OF MATRIMONY

have accordingly been admitted to that degree with all honors,

rights and privileges belonging thereto.

Awarded this _____ day of _____, 19 _____.

stands for *groom* and look at how the love of a bride and groom, or any married couple, can form a bridge for a happy life together.

Love is a bridge that spans otherwise impossible crossings. Love works at changing a "me first" attitude into a "we" outlook. It bridges the gap of misunderstandings by assuming the best possible motive behind actions that offend. Love talks out feelings before they fester.

Love will realize that irritability and impatience often have nothing personally to do with one's mate. Love will comfort and sympathize or allow the distressed partner to be alone for a while to overcome the outside pressures that probably led to the explosion.

Love will bridge the pride problem when each partner lifts the mate to the number one position. Everyone needs to march at the head of someone's parade, and honor bestowed does not demand rank.

Because love is patient, it will enable a couple to wait until they can afford to purchase an expensive item. Love will consider the money needs of the partner. Love will lead a couple to consult each other before making any big investment of money. Love will thus prevent money problems and forgive if one partner should slip occasionally.

Love comes to grip with the busy bustle of life. It overcomes the neglect problem by learning to say no to some of the outside forces that rob a couple of each other's companionship.

Love desires to be with the loved one but also allows the mate breathing room for some hobbies and friends. Love participates in some outside interests and at other times joyfully frees the mate to be with others.

Love bridges the in-law hassle by converting relatives-in-law to relatives-in-love. After all, it was love, not law, that brought those relatives into family relationship. Mel Johnson of "Tips for Teens" says, "Love reduces friction to a fraction."

The *Living Bible* states: "Love is very patient and kind, never jealous or envious, never boastful or proud, never haughty or selfish or rude. Love does not demand its own way. It is not irritable or touchy. It does not hold grudges and will hardly even notice when others do it wrong. It is never glad about injustice, but rejoices whenever truth wins out. If you love someone you will be loyal to him no matter what the cost. You will always believe in him, always expect the best of him, and always stand your ground in defending him . . . love goes on forever" (1 Corinthians 13:4-8). "Let love be your greatest aim" (1 Corinthians 14:1).

On Love

Love is a bridge
    that covers the murky waters below—
        the Waters riled up with Misunderstanding,
                    Impatience,
                    Contempt.

Love is enduring.
    The waters are calm, and overhead
    THE BRIDGE STANDS FIRM.

(Dee Gronhovd)

This kind of love comes from God. When your love bridge gets shaky, PRAY!

This devotional thought can easily be developed into a decorating scheme by doing the following: Paint in pastels, or watercolors, a wall-sized nature scene with a bridge over a fast-running stream and a couple standing on the bridge. If no one in the group is an artist, the mural could easily be done by tracing a picture of a bridge with a couple onto a clear sheet of acetate. (If such a picture isn't available, super-impose a couple from another picture onto a bridge scene.) Place the acetate sheet on an overhead projector borrowed from church or school and project the scene on a paper or cloth banner on the wall. Trace your scene with a pencil, pen, or marker and paint or chalk the color on it.

This scene could be kept and used again—perhaps for a youth sweetheart banquet.

Use the bridge decorating idea on the anniversary cake also.

Links of Love

To prepare for the program, cut 20 strips of construction paper (10 inches by 1 inch) in the theme colors. Write one of the following words and references on each strip, alternating colors:

1. Commitment (Psalm 37:5)
2. Love (1 John 4:7)
3. Praise (Psalm 106:1)
4. Kindness (Ephesians 4:32)
5. Contentment (Philippians 4:11)
6. Peace (Philippians 4:7)
7. Communication (Ecclesiastes 3:7)
8. Prayer (Colossians 4:2)
9. Harmony (Philippians 4:2)
10. Positive Thoughts (Philippians 4:8)
11. Encouragement (Hebrews 3:13 NASB)
12. Hospitality (Hebrews 13:2)
13. Trust (Proverbs 31:11)
14. Forgiving (Matthew 6:12)
15. Enjoy (1 Timothy 6:17)
16. Rejoicing (Philippians 4:4)
17. Trials (Romans 5:3)

During the presentation, you will need one person to glue or tape the construction paper strips together into the links of a chain as each word is talked about and its accompanying verse is read. Others should be asked to read the verses. (Each verse could be typed on a separate slip of paper and given in advance to the person who will read it).

Speaker: A big ocean consists of tiny drops of water. Our lives are filled with the little incidents of each day that go to make up our characters. If we allow our lives to be cluttered with meaningless moments, we will one day come to realize the results of our lives are just that—meaningless.

Now is the time to add an abundance of happy thoughts, positive actions and all the pleasantries that go to make up an abundant life. We have been watching _____ and _____ as they have been forging links of love for _____ years. As we meet to celebrate with them on

18

their _____ anniversary it will do us all good to scrutinize some of these links in their chain of love.

I've asked many of you to help in forming a chain to refresh us on the love links of life.

(You might want to personalize the following comments by including incidents from the couple's life.)

The first link in their strong chain of love is *commitment*. They are committed to God and to each other.

(The person forming the chain tapes the construction paper strip that reads commitment *into a ring. Someone else reads Psalm 37:5.)*

Link two is *love*. As important as that was at the beginning of their marriage, it is even more important now.

(The strip that reads love *should be looped through the first ring and then taped into a second ring, forming the first two links of a chain. Someone reads 1 John 4:7. The pattern continues after each of the following words.)*

Praise is a vital link. _____ and _____ praise God. They are also generous with praise to and for each other.

Kindness forms a strong link, one that smooths out rough spots in their marriage.

Contentment is a by-product of kindness.

We see *peace* in your home.

The link of *communication* continues to develop.

Prayer is a strong link in your love.

Harmony is sweet as you unite in the Lord.

Positive thoughts forge enduring links of love.

You exhort and *encourage* each other when life gets tedious and difficult.

You remember to show *hospitality*.

The link of *trust* is firm between you.

A *forgiving* spirit dwells within you both.

The link of your *rejoicing* is a joy for us to behold.

Trials, too, have forged a link in your love chain. We have all heard that a chain is only as strong as its weakest link. Trials make the links already forged more durable. We need not shy away from the fires of trials because they purify the links of love and turn them into gold that will not rust away.

19

The links in the chain of love will endure forever. "The fruit of the Spirit is love, joy, peace, patience, kindness, goodness, faithfulness, gentleness, self-control" (Galatians 5:22-23).

We thank you, _____ and _____, for your example of love in action. We want to follow your example.

Decorate the hall with hearts and flowers. On one wall put two large lacy hearts with a picture of one of the marriage partners on each one. Or post one large heart with a picture of the couple in the center. When the chain is completed, drape it between the two hearts, or form the chain into a giant heart on the wall around the single fancy heart.

Renewal of Vows Ceremony

Pastor conducting ceremony: Happy is the day when a man and woman come together to renew their sacred covenant of marriage. God looks with kindly favor upon this sacred covenant made between a husband and wife.

    (Lead in a prayer.)

    (husband), will you now receive *(wife)* as your wife, to continue to build a home together under God, to continue to give yourself fully in the sacred relationship of husband and wife? Will you continue to freely give her your love? Will you continue to respect her? Be honest with her? Stand by her, comfort her, watch over her, whether she is sick or enjoying good health? Will you continue to remain free of all others?

Husband answers: I will.

Pastor: *(wife)*, will you now receive *(husband)* as your husband, to continue to build a home together under God, to continue to give yourself fully in the sacred relationship of husband and wife? Will you continue to freely give him your love? Will you continue to respect him? Be honest with him? Stand by him, comfort him, watch over him, whether he is sick or enjoying good health? Will you continue to remain free of all others?

Wife answers: I will.

20

Pastor: _(husband)_ and _(wife)_, will you now face each other, join hands and repeat after me?

I, _(husband)_, receive you, _(wife)_, as a gift from God. I joyfully receive you to continue as my partner in life, to have and to care for from this day forward, in times of sorrow and in times of happiness, in times of poverty and in times of prosperity, in times of sickness and in times of well-being, to love and to enjoy, till death makes us separate. I again pledge my love to you this day.

(Wife then repeats these vows.)

When God made a covenant with Noah, he set a rainbow in the clouds and said, "I will look upon it that I may remember that it is an everlasting covenant." _____ years ago you chose rings as tokens of your marriage covenant. They are made of a metal that is not easily tarnished and one that endures. These rings are an endless circle, unless broken by an outside force, and are a symbol of the unbroken marital union, which God has established.

(husband), will you place this ring on _(wife's)_ hand and repeat after me: With this ring I assure you of the depth of my continuing love, and all my worldly goods I share, in the name of the Father, and of the Son, and of the Holy Spirit.

(Wife then repeats this to husband.)

Let us bow our heads in the attitude of prayer.

(Have an appropriate song here.)

I, along with this group of people, wish for you, _(husband)_ and _(wife)_, happiness, success, and God's blessings as you continue on your journey through life together.

(Couple kiss.)

A Grand Affair

For a fiftieth (or later) anniversary, enlist the grandchildren to provide most of the memories and program content. Assign them well in advance some or all of the following topics:

1. My first recollections of Grandma and Grandpa
2. Visits to Grandma's

3. Lessons learned there
4. Shopping trips with them
5. Games, fun times, and feelings
6. Smells at Grandma's
7. Traditions we shared

Ask them to speak a few minutes on these and other big moments in their memories of grandparents.

If some are musical, ask them to perform as Grandma and Grandpa often requested when they were growing up.

Grandchildren may also wish to display items they gave their grandparents or their grandparents gave them.

Make a poster or an acetate cell for an overhead projector of this acrostic:[2]

Grandparents are:

G reeters, givers, gems, and game-players
R avers, rejoicers, responders, rewarders
A dmirers, attic-fillers, anecdote-tellers,
    aid-and-abetters
N eat, necessities, notable, nestlers
D ears and diplomats, doers and doctors—and let's all
    hope they're durable!

Add other appropriate or personalized adjectives.

Have a grandchild read this acrostic as concluding comments.

DECORATIONS

Basics

Crepe paper and candles are friends indeed to the decorating chairman. They team up to camouflage and beautify the drabbest of surroundings. Both come in a wide variety of hues and thus fit into almost any color scheme.

Learn the couple's wedding colors and general decorating theme and use crepe paper in those colors to accent a special spot or disguise an eyesore. Twist, drape, or ruffle it into archways, canopies, frames, or backdrops. Paper an entire

2. Acrostic idea came from Audrey Ouhl.

wall with a luscious background color. Spread your wishes with pre-cut, preprinted "Happy Anniversary" crepe paper banners that can be purchased at most stationery stores, or make your own.

Decorating themes can be geared to the month in which the anniversary occurs: January, snowmen; February, red hearts; March, shamrocks; April, umbrella and flowers; May, maypole; June, bride dolls; July, flags; August, vacation theme; September, back-to-school theme; October, harvest; November, Thanksgiving; December, Christmas decorations.

If the couple has no particular color choices, the stone for the anniversary year might lend a decorating idea for color on the cake and room decor. For example, the ruby is the stone suggested for the fortieth anniversary. Ruby red accents could brighten a fortieth celebration.

Decorations for an anniversary celebration need not be elaborate but should be imaginative, appropriate, and personalized. Many types of items can be purchased; others may require a bit of creative skill to assemble.

Some of the ready-to-use decorations available at most party supply stores are: gold and silver banners that wish "Happy Anniversary," fringed "Congratulations" banners, 9-feet-long white honeycomb tissue bell garlands trimmed with silver or gold, personalized bell banners with a letter on each bell, streamers of 12 honeycomb bells (in pastel shades) attached to a white satin ribbon, individual honeycomb tissue bells of various sizes and colors, small satin bells in pastel colors, honeycomb bell clusters, tiny gold and silver bells, doves with honeycomb tissue bodies, large cotton and feather doves with movable wings, large and small anniversary wreaths in silver and gold, dated (25, 30, 35, 40, 45, 50) anniversary wreaths, various cardboard and tissue centerpieces, large dated floral wreath with candleholders, "Happy Anniversary" balloons, heart-shaped balloons, and silver and gold balloons.

These store bought items can be draped on walls, around windows and tables or even a large punch bowl. When combined with crepe paper and a little creativity, a few purchased items can be used again and again to make each celebration different.

Nutcups

Nutcups add such a festive note to any celebration; do include them. If you wish to buy them you can usually find a good selection for sale.

Some of those might include: swans, fluted foil nutcups in colors or silver and gold, gold and silver foil shell nutcups, small loving cups, small gold baskets, mortarboard nutcups, and small heart-shaped boxes.

If you prefer to, you could make some that cost little more than time and energy in small amounts.

Star cups. Buy star-shaped ribbon bows in pretty colors. Glue miniature foil or bonbon cups in the center of the bow. These cups are tiny and hold few calorie-filled nuts but are so dainty and pretty.

Garden varieties. From the lowly egg carton you can make a variety of garden flowers. Using the colored styrofoam cartons, shape the cups to make Pastel Pinks, Blue Bells, Lily Whites, Jaunty Jonquils, Bright Buttercups, or Bells of Ireland. The color of the egg carton largely determines the choice of which flower you make.

Look at a picture of each of the flowers named above. With scissors trim the upper edge of the individual cups from the carton to resemble the petal shapes. Glue the cup to a small square of cardboard and you have pretty posies to transform a plain table into a lovely garden.

Differentiate between the jonquils and buttercups by placing a small white or gold lacy doily between the egg cup and the cardboard for jonquils.

Choose your flowered nutcups to coordinate with the couple's colors. Or for a springtime canopy of color use several kinds of flowers on the same table.

Cool Candles

Egg cartons can also be used to make a candle no fire chief could be concerned about.

Choose white or pastel-colored styrofoam egg cartons. Eight cartons are needed for each candle.

Remove the lid and tab fasteners from each carton. With a sharp knife or razor blade, cut each carton lengthwise to make two long cup sections of 6 cups each. Round off and trim 1/2 inch from the inside cut edge. Poke a hole in the bottom cup and the top cup of each section.

Insert a 6-inch-long elastic cord through the top holes of each section, connecting the cartons so that they are stacked inside one another. Tie the cord as tightly as possible. Repeat this process through the bottom holes.

Carefully fan the stacked segments apart so they form a rounded candle shape with the uncut edges on the outside.

Decorate the candle with glitter. Insert and glue a red or orange fake fur flame into the top end of the candle. Glue the bottom end onto a round 6-inch (or larger) styrofoam base.

Finish the base with ribbon around the outer edge and greenery and flowers poked into the base surrounding the candle.

Banners

For personalized banners, make your own squared letters or overlapping balloon letters. Adjust the patterns below to desired size and cut your message from poster board, tissue paper, foil or construction paper. Add sparkle with glitter if you wish.

For squared letters, you need one rectangle of paper, each the same size, for each letter. The outer edges of the paper will be the size of each letter. Cut as illustrated by the dotted lines. Y, W, V, T, M, I, and A will be more uniform if paper is folded vertically with edges even. Cut as illustrated by dotted lines.

To make double letters hinged at the top to hang over ribbon or string, use rectangles twice the height you want the letters to be. Fold this rectangle in half horizontally with top and lower edges together. Cut as with single squared letters with top edges of the letters on the fold.

Happy Anniversary

Silver Golden

0123456789

25TH

Congratulations

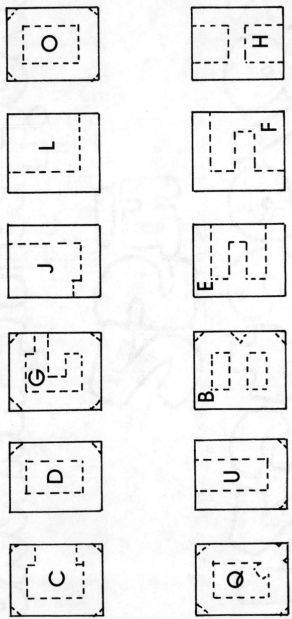

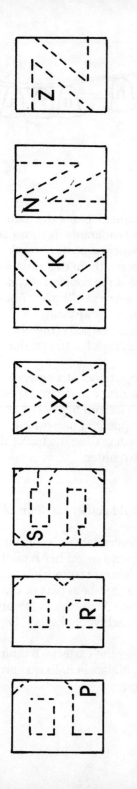
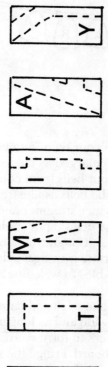

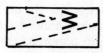
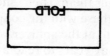
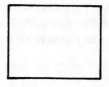

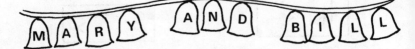

Make your own "names in bells banner." Using the pattern above (enlarged as big as needed for readability in your party room), cut bells from construction paper or poster board. Letter the bells as illustrated, then fasten them to a ribbon or crepe paper streamer and drape across the room or a wall.

(These bell shapes could also be used to say "Happy Anniversary," "Congratulations," "Welcome," or any other appropriate message. Other shapes besides bells could be used: Bibles to welcome a new pastor, caps for the graduate, etc.)

To make a fringed banner: Cut crepe paper streamers 6 inches wide and as long as needed to drape in desired spot. Cut letters to form words 4 inches high from heavy foil or poster board. Fringe the streamer, clipping at narrow intervals up 3 1/2 inches from the lower edge. Glue the top of the letters to the unclipped edge of the streamer.

Personalized Party

Another simple decoration idea could center on items of personal importance to the couple.

Has your honoree kept all her anniversary cards during the years? Ask her daughter or a close friend to get her reminiscing over them. Then "sneak out" a favorite from each year. Share these with the couple and their guests as part of the program at the anniversary celebration. If they've celebrated too many years to read a card from each year, display them all and read just a few.

You may choose, instead, to arrange the cards on a table or wall to form a large heart with their initials in it. Extra cards could form the year of their anniversary.

Money Tree

Purchase or make a money tree for your celebrants. Spray paint a tree branch white, gold, or silver. Mount it into a plant pot weighted with plaster of paris. Collect money in advance or invite guests to come prepared to tie or hang money on the tree. Tie bells on the branches with yarn or ribbon of the couple's colors. Tape ribbon or yarn to silver dollars and then secure the ribbon to the branches.

Your money tree can be an attractive mixture of bills and coins to help the couple take a second honeymoon or for any use they wish. A gold tree with all silver dollars would be appropriate to a silver wedding anniversary.

Keep records of the donors and the amount, if you wish, so the couple can express appreciation.

Wishing Well

A variation of the money tree is a "wishing you well" wishing well. Construct a small wishing well from an ice cream or chicken bucket. Glue brick- or rock-patterned crepe paper around it. Fasten two dowel sticks upright to support a cardboard "shingled" roof. Put the well in a conspicuous place for guests to drop in a monetary wish if they desire.

A larger well could be constructed for the receiving of "wishing you well" cards. The couple would enjoy these in private after the guests depart.

Gift Tables

In decorating, provisions should be made for a place to receive and display gifts. You can open the gifts before the celebration begins and display them on a table. Or the couple can open the gifts themselves after the celebration. If you choose to open gifts at the celebration, prepare for an interesting receptacle to receive them, someone to record who gave what, and someone else to arrange them on a display table after they're opened.

Invite guests to put gifts that aren't too heavy in a gondola balloon. Borrow a real one if you have hot air enthusiasts around. Or hang a large wicker basket (this could be a gift also) about waist high from ropes attached to the ceiling.

Suspend a colorful beach ball over it to represent the balloon. Label the gondola "High Flying Futures."

As an alternate gift arrangement, stand a large doll couple (bride and groom dolls or street-clothed boy and girl dolls) on a table with a child's umbrella closed at their feet. Hang a shiny "sun" over their heads and the caption "We Wish You Sunny Days Ahead."

Are your honorees planning a boat trip abroad? Receive their gifts in a make-shift love boat. Attach heart-shaped sails to a two man canoe to wish them "smooth sailing" in the years ahead.

Your decorating theme may suggest some other interesting way of collecting the gifts. Use a prettily draped or skirted table if nothing else is available.

POEMS

On a Friend's Anniversary

Amid your many friends
    'Neath a shaded lamp's soft ray,
You are tenderly reviving
    Mem'ries of your Wedding Day;
When you truly pledged each other
    Love throughout life's earthly span;
Hand in hand you took your journey
    Into love's delightful land.

One by one you've passed the milestones,
    Swiftly they have glided past,
Years of sun, and rain, and shadow,
    Some by storm-clouds overcast;
Gone, at times, the rosy splendor
    Of your first fantastic dreams,
But in place, an understanding
    Of what true love really means.

For true love but clings the closer
    When the storm-clouds hover o'er,
And the hands clasp more securely
    In the dark days, than before.
And the tears that dimmed your vision
    Do not seem to pain you so,
As you trace the lovely rainbow
    In the sunset's afterglow.

Shall we not then thank the Father
    Who sends sunshine after rain?
That through all the lights and shadows
    He remains the very same?
And when friend and lover leave us,
    We may still cling to His hand,
He who says, "Lo I am with you,
    Even to the journey's end."

(Emma P. Jule)

This Thing Called Love

"This wonderful thing called Love!" we exclaim,
And yet to define it, we try all in vain.
This thing so elusive, and yet all so real,
So tender and fervent in its sweet appeal.

Why can't we define it, why can't we explain
What it consists of? Why, love is so plain!
Still we can't find a word to encircle the whole
Of love in its moods and its phases untold.

And yet, it is simple, as simple can be
For love lives a lifetime; and how then can we
(Poor human beings) expect to make plain
In one single word, what a lifetime contains?

Love is a look, a glance, or a gesture,
Clothed in a radiant, enchanting vesture,
Dreaming sweet dreams full of visions that please,
With no fears for tomorrow's realities.

Love is a cord, a cord strong and steady,
That securely holds, and keeps the heart ready
For joy or for sorrow, for sickness or health—
We cannot exhaust the supply of love's wealth.

Love cherishes laughter, and sunshine, and cheer,
Love sees but the rainbow, forgets all the tears;
It sheds a bright halo of immortal light
That lives for us, bears with us, covers our blight.

33

For love does not change with the passing of years.
Real love is lasting—it only reveres
That precious companion, when youth's morn is past,
Love sees no changes, its sweetness still lasts.

(Emma P. Jule)

If I Had Only Known

If I'd known what I know now,
Before I said my vow,
I'd saved a sea of tears
And wrinkles on my brow . . .

If I'd known this, in the past:
That honeymoons don't last,
And that husbands do have faults,
That grocery bills are vast . . .

I had simply not been told
That formulas grow cold,
That babies have no scruples,
And midnight cries get old . . .

Oh that I had only known
Of ignorance, my own,
Of daily stress and strife, and
Of children, mischief-prone . . .

That no child stays cute and small,
That, growing up, they fall,
That they seem to need us less,
Nor answer beck and call . . .

No, I wasn't quite prepared
For all that I have fared.
If I'd known the price so high,
The task I'd never dared.

But I'm glad I didn't know
The row that I would hoe.
I could have wept in vain, and
For wrinkles, nothing show.

34

Scalding tears must come somehow
And wrinkles to the brow.
Why waste them, then, on less than
The best life can endow?

(Betty Jo Mathis)[3]

For Better or for Worse?

Long years ago our lives we pledged
Each to the other, neither hedged;
Excited, eager, giving all.
The world was ours—we'd never fall.

We'd not be sick, for we were strong.
We'd not be poor—(for very long)!
There'd be no worse—only better;
For we were young—none could deter.

Years have passed and young hopes shattered,
Leaving only things that mattered.
Fame was transient, health elusive,
Wealth deceptive, dreams delusive.

But love has grown, faith has strengthened;
Views have mellowed, vision lengthened.
And we have learned the lesson well
That marriage vows have much to tell.

For not success nor even wealth,
Nor fortune's smile nor perfect health
Assure a marriage that won't fail;
A couple needs the storm and gale.

Shattered dreams and dampened feather
Drive a couple close together;
And weakened health and empty purse
Reveal the better, not the worse.

(Betty Jo Mathis)[4]

3. From *Spider in the Palace*, by Betty Jo Mathis. Used by permission.
4. From *Spider in the Palace*, by Betty Jo Mathis. Used by permission.

35

Too Late Now

Too busy to think of divorce
Too poor to pay the judge
Too blind to worldly ways
Too childish to hold a grudge

Too many bruises to comfort
Too many tears to dry
Too many pants to change
Too many a trusting eye

Too many hilarious jokes
Too many trials to share
Too many lives at stake
Too many a friend to care

Too many, the patch-up quarrels
Too much joy for a scowl
Too many grandkids now
Too late to throw in the towel!!

(Betty Jo Mathis)[5]

10th

Ten years together. Can it be
A whole decade has gone
Since you pledged to eternity
The love that made you one?
Ten years indeed! And blest has been
The way o'er which you've trod:
And, oh, what wonders you have seen,
Wrought by the hand of God.
And though your love was sweet the day
When first you pledged your troth,
It has grown sweeter all the way,
More precious to you both.
New heights and depths of Love Divine
Have blended with your own,
Filling your inmost souls with joy
Before to you unknown.

(Avis B. Christiansen)[6]

(Substitute any number of years for "ten" to fit your situation.)

5. From *Spider in the Palace*, by Betty Jo Mathis. Used by permission.
6. From *Food for the Body, for the Soul*, by Avis B. Christiansen (Chicago: Moody Press, 1943).

25th

A quarter of a century you've walked life's way together,
Through joy and sorrow, loss and gain, and through all kinds of
    weather;
And as you've shared its pain and grief, as well as many a
    blessing,
You've found your gladness more complete, your sadness less
    distressing.
For love can tinge the darkest cloud with glints of heavenly
    sweetness,
And add to e'en our deepest joys a sense of rich completeness.
So on this silver wedding day life holds a fuller meaning
Than e'er it did in by-gone hours of wishful, empty dreaming.
Your Father's hand hath never failed in any time of trial,
And never when His help you've sought have you met stern
    denial.
Today with hearts still undismayed, you face the unknown
    morrow,
Strong in His might, and unafraid of turmoil, pain or sorrow.

(Avis B. Christiansen)[7]

50th

Golden thoughts come stealing
Down memory's land today
As on this fiftieth milestone
You linger on your way.
And as a curtain lifted,
The past is brought to view,—
The happy days and hours
Which long ago you knew.
The dear forgotten faces
Again you seem to see;
Old songs, old friends, old places
Pass by in memory.
Life's sun will soon be setting,—
The thought brings naught of pain,
For in yon Land of Gladness
There waits eternal gain.
Dear ones await up yonder
Whom you have missed so long,

7. From *Food for the Body, for the Soul*, by Avis B. Christiansen (Chicago:
Moody Press, 1943).

37

And oft you long to mingle
With that triumphant throng.
But deeper far the yearning
To see His kindly face.
Who through the years has loved you,
And saved you by His grace.

(Avis B. Christiansen)[8]

A Change of Heart

I loved you on our wedding day
    Which seems now long and far away.
I longed to spend my life with you
    I loved you then, for love was new.

But now some twenty years have fled—
    Thru' tears and trials our path has led.
The strains and stress have done their part
    To cause a change within my heart.

This change in me you know is true
    For I've confessed it oft to you.
Love as when we wed? No—Never!
    Today I love you more than ever.

(Betty Jo Mathis)[9]

Second Honeymoon

"Oh, for a chance," I often pined,
"to leave this noisy gang behind
to chat with you, uninterrupted,
our peace and quiet not corrupted . . ."
Just two of us—my spouse and I
For such a treat my heart did sigh.

At last our chance did come along.
We left the kids with cheery song.
Our second honeymoon'd begun—
The two of us would have some fun!
No childish quarrels to referee—
The whole front seat for me and thee.

8. From *Food for the Body, for the Soul,* by Avis B. Christiansen (Chicago: Moody Press, 1943).
9. From *Common to Man,* by Betty Jo Mathis. Used by permission.

No urgent stops at service stations,
No squabbles over candy rations,
No sticky fingers on the dash,
No bottles, pins or diaper rash,
No humid breathing down our backs,
No student driver's smart wisecracks.

What luxury, what calm, what lush!
(What stretched-out miles,
    what morbid hush!)
The kids back home,
    we thought about 'em—
It sure was lonely there without 'em.
We turned the radio up loud
    to keep the silence down,
And jumped whene'er we heard
    a familiar, childish sound.

Our second honeymoon was fine,
    'twas nice to get away.
But it's good to be back home
    and enjoy a hectic day.
Next honeymoon we take,
    there'll be children in our midst—
How did we e'er enjoy the first
    without a load of kids?

(Betty Jo Mathis)[10]

Great to be in Love

Oh, it's great to be in love,
When you're young and full of pep,
When your skies are clear above,
And you walk with bouyant step;
When you feel you've got it made
And your world is bright and green,
When one's a gay young blade
And the other's just a teen.

It's great to hear 'your song,'
And meander, holding hands,
So sure that nothing wrong
Could dim your future plans.

10. From *Common to Man*, by Betty Jo Mathis. Used by permission.

When your wedding rings still gleam
And life looks bright and gay,
When you share your fondest dreams
And laughter greets each day.

But it's great to be in love
When the years have left their mark;
And your hair is thin above
And you've sorta lost your spark;
When your bank account is drained
And your arms are full of babies,
When your confidence has waned,
Your 'yesses' turned to 'maybes.'

It's great to get a thrill
When you hear that step again,
To feel your heart stand still
As you trade a knowing grin.
It's great to get a hug
Tho' you're out of shape and lumpy,
To feel secure and snug
Tho' fashion says you're dumpy;

When your wedding ring's worn thru
And your hands are gnarled and rough,
When your dreams have not come true,
And walking makes you puff.
It's great to have a song,
Tho' your own is out of style,
It's great to tag along
And enjoy each other's smile.

It's great to be in love
In spite of trials and tears,
To fit like hand in glove,
To be mellowed by the years.
It's great to be in love,
With your hearts so firmly set,
That when beckoned up above,
You part with no regret.

(Betty Jo Mathis)[11]

11. From *Of Throne and Footstool,* by Betty Jo Mathis. Used by permission.

What Every Husband Ought to Know

Some things don't improve with age. Wives are an exception. The longer they are married, the better, as a rule, they become.

A ten year old automobile is ready for the junk pile. Its gloss is gone; it creaks and squeaks; its performance is faulty and it costs too much to have it overhauled. Some men think wives are like that. Since it is illegal to throw a wife on a junk pile, they dispose of her in some more orderly manner and get a new model.

But they are wrong. A wife is not like an automobile. Ten years after saying, "I do," she is just beginning to show her worth. Every year after that she gets better and more useful to her husband. After 15 or 20 years she may need an occasional repaint job, but she is certainly worth it. After 25 years a wife becomes indispensable. She may not look as glossy, but she has more under the hood.

The buttons she sews on stay on longer.

She may still believe that money grows on trees, but she realizes that kind of tree doesn't grow in your backyard.

When she occasionally has to carry the garbage out, she doesn't make a federal case out of it.

If she finds a blond hair on your coat, she doesn't make a big scene. She knows that some dog just brushed against you.

She no longer yells about going home to Mother if you overdo anything. Her biggest threat is, "I'll tell the doctor on you!"

The meals she fixes don't taste like a misprint in the bachelor cookbook.

If her vacuum cleaner breaks down, she fixes it herself.

In a pinch, she'll dip into her secret emergency fund and lend a husband a little extra. (You can never expect this from young wives; they're always broke.)

Yes, it takes a lot of time, trouble and understanding for a husband to take a flibberty-gibbity young bride and turn her into man's greatest masterpiece—a perfect wife, nobly planned. But in what more rewarding manner can a fellow spend his years?

(Author Unknown)

Prayer for a Bride and Groom

O God of love, Thou hast established marriage for the welfare and happiness of mankind. Thine was the plan and only with

Thee can we work it out with joy. Thou hast said, "It is not good for man to be alone. I will make a help meet for him." Now our joys are doubled since the happiness of one is the happiness of the other. Our burdens are now halved when we share them; we divide the load.

Bless this husband. Bless him as provider of nourishment and raiment and sustain him in all the exactions and pressures of his battle for bread. May his strength be her protection, his character be her boast and her pride, and may he so live that she will find in him the haven for which the heart of woman truly longs.

Bless this loving wife. Give her tenderness that will make her great, a deep sense of understanding and a great faith in Thee. Give her that inner beauty of soul that never fades, that eternal youth that is found in holding fast the things that never age.

Teach them that marriage is not living merely for each other; it is two uniting and joining hands to serve Thee. Give them a great spiritual purpose in life. May they seek the kingdom of God and His righteousness, and the other things shall be added unto them.

May they not expect that perfection of each other that belongs only to Thee. May they minimize each other's weaknesses, be swift to praise and magnify each other's points of comeliness and strength, and see each other through a lover's kind and patient eyes.

Now make such assignments to them on the scroll of Thy will as will bless them and develop their characters as they walk together. Give them enough tears to keep them tender, enough hurts to keep them humane, enough of failure to keep their hands clenched tightly in Thine, and enough success to make them sure they walk with God.

May they never take each other's love for granted, but always experience that breathless wonder that exclaims, "Out of all this world you have chosen me."

When life is done and the sun is setting, may they be found then as now hand in hand, still thanking God for each other. May they serve Thee happily, faithfully, together, until at last one shall lay the other into the arms of God.

This we ask through Jesus Christ, great lover of our souls. Amen.

(Louis H. Evans)[12]

12. Reprinted by permission of the American Tract Society, Garland, Texas.

2
Church Celebrations

This chapter includes ideas for church dedications, anniversaries, and mortgage burning ceremonies. Many of the ideas are interchangeable or could be used on other church occasions as well.

CHURCH DEDICATION

Plan a program of music and Scripture around the actual prayer of dedication. The pastor or a leader of your denomination should give a short sermon. Reminiscings about the beginning and progress of the work would be most appropriate together with much giving of thanks.

Recognize people who have donated skilled labor and materials to the building. You may want to present plaques to those who have made outstanding contributions. Don't forget, however, to give God the glory for what has been accomplished.

If the celebration is in the afternoon, serve a light supper to your guests. If it is held in the evening, simple refreshments would be appropriate.

Of course, give all guests a guided tour of the new facilities.

Possible church dedication themes are:

Launch out into the deep
I have set before you an open door
To God be the glory
For this we thank thee
What hath God wrought!

We Give Thee but Thine Own

Speaker: We read David's prayer in 1 Chronicles 29 as he
prepared the materials for his son Solomon to use in the
building of the great Temple of the Lord. David was overwhelmed by the sacrifice and cooperation of his people.
"Then the people rejoiced because they had offered so
willingly, for they made their offering to the Lord with a
whole heart; and King David also rejoiced greatly" (1
Chronicles 29:9).

You have also sacrificed with a whole heart to make our
building a reality. We rejoice today as King David did. *(At
this point you can mention individuals who performed
specific tasks or companies that donated materials and
thank them.)*

David here praises the Lord for His greatness, His
majesty and His dominion over all. He acknowledges
God's omnipotence. He also acknowledges Him as the
giver of every good and perfect gift. David is overwhelmed
with gratitude to God as he thinks about the privilege of
being a worker together with Him. Only because He had
given first could David and his people give back to Him for
this great endeavor of building a Temple to the Lord.

We, too, acknowledge today that what we have given to
build our church came from God in the first place. As the
songwriter wrote, "We give Thee but Thine own." Like
David, we rejoice today because we were able to give of
our money and our time to build this building for God to
be a light in this community and draw people to Him. We
thank Him for giving us the means to give and the ability
to do so. What a privilege it is to be a worker together with

Him. "For we are God's fellow-workers" (1 Corinthians 3:9).

We dedicate this building to His glory, the salvation of souls, and the edification of the believers. Our desire is that we will not only reach out to our community with the message of the gospel but also to the ends of the earth. For this purpose we now dedicate our building to the Lord.

Scripture Reading

How lovely is your Temple, O Lord of the armies of heaven.

I long, yes, faint with longing to be able to enter your court-yard and come near to the Living God. Even the sparrows and swallows are welcome to come and nest among your altars and there have their young, O Lord of heaven's armies, my King and my God! How happy are those who can live in your Temple singing your praises.

Happy are those who are strong in the Lord, who want above all else to follow your steps. When they walk through the Valley of Weeping it will become a place of springs where pools of blessing and refreshment collect after rains: They will grow constantly in strength and each of them is invited to meet with the Lord in Zion . . . .

A single day spent in your Temple is better than a thousand anywhere else: I would rather be a doorman of the Temple of my God than live in palaces of wickedness. For Jehovah God is our Light and our Protector. He gives us grace and glory. No good thing will he withhold from those who walk along his paths.

O Lord of the armies of heaven, blessed are those who trust in you.

(Psalm 84, *Living Bible*)

DECORATIONS

You will not need to do much decorating for this event. The new church itself is what is on display. Banners announcing your theme are appropriate. The figure of Christ holding your church would make a beautiful picture for your dedication bulletin or for a wall poster.

Flowers or greenery would enhance the beauty of your church and make the occasion more festive.

CHURCH ANNIVERSARY

Who Is in Charge?

Select a church anniversary committee at least a year in advance of your celebration. This will allow time for them to prayerfully plan this very special time for your congregation.

A church anniversary is made special by pictures depicting the church's growth. If you are fortunate enough to have colored slides or movies, show them during your celebration. Also display snapshots showing the progress of the church through the years. You can arrange these on colorful posters or in albums.

Every church should have a competent historian who sees to it that significant pictures are taken and put into albums. Also included in the albums should be newspaper clippings about the church: its dedication, additions made, new pastors coming, any outstanding feats of its members, and so on.

Who Is Invited?

Invite all church members and friends, of course, as well as the public. Also invite former pastors and wives as well as pastors in nearby churches.

What Do You Do?

Some churches schedule a week of special meetings in connection with their anniversary celebration. The event starts with a banquet carrying out a suitable theme such as "To God be the glory." The former pastors take turns speaking at the evening services until the last Sunday when the celebration is climaxed by a potluck supper and a special anniversary program.

Possible church anniversary themes are:

> To God be the glory
> For this we thank Thee
> What hath God wrought!
> Not one word has failed
> Forget none of His benefits
> Remember all the way that He has led

Remember

Speaker: Remembering is an important part of the Christian walk. Throughout the Bible, God urges His people to remember. Peter in writing his second epistle says, "This is now, beloved, the second letter I am writing to you in which I am stirring up your sincere mind by way of reminder" (2 Peter 3:1). He then goes on to urge them to remember what they have been taught.

Moses urged the Israelites to remember. They were to recall what the Lord did for them in Egypt, how He brought them out of bondage and through the Red Sea while their enemies were destroyed. They were also to remember all the ways the Lord had led them in the wilderness for forty years, how the Lord fed them with manna and provided water to drink, how He kept their clothing from wearing out, how He taught them and disciplined them and brought them safely to the borders of the Promised Land.

When Jesus instituted the Lord's Supper, He told His disciples to eat the bread and drink the cup "in remembrance of Me." They were to remember His death as they looked forward to His return.

Today is a time of remembering for us. As individual Christians we remember the time we came to the Savior to receive His salvation. That deliverance from sin and the world was even greater than Israel's deliverance from Egypt, which typifies it. As a congregation we remember the beginning of our church.

(Reminisce here about how the church was started. Invite several charter members to speak of the beginnings.)
As the Israelites were to remember all the ways the Lord had led them, let us today remember how God has led us.

(Have one or several church members tell of God's leading since the early beginnings. You may want to assign specific time periods to each one; for instance, 1950-1960. Or you may want to assign specific events. Encourage them to tell what happened in the church during those years. Was remodeling done on the building or an addition com-

pleted? Did you add a youth pastor or a Christian education director? Were souls saved? Was it a time of growth? Did you pass through a time of difficulty?)

Moses told the Israelites, "You shall remember all the way which the Lord your God has led you in the wilderness these forty years, that He might humble you, testing you, to know what was in your heart, whether you would keep His commandments or not" (Deuteronomy 8:2).

We realize that improvements of our facilities, added staff and growth in church members are not the most important way that He has led us. We must also remember how He has taught us and brought spiritual growth to us as individuals and as a group.

(Give opportunity for individuals to tell of spiritual blessings and lessons learned during the past years in the church. This may include failures that brought humility and a drawing near to God as well as spiritual victories.)

End this part of the program with a song of praise such as "To God Be the Glory" or "Praise Him" and a time of thanksgiving in prayer.

His Benefits

Speaker: In Psalm 103:1-2 we read: "Bless the Lord, O my soul; and all that is within me, bless His holy name. Bless the Lord, O my soul, and forget none of His benefits." These verses remind us that we are to be specific not only in our praying but also in our praising.

Today we are celebrating the _____ anniversary of our church. We realize that it is only because of God's grace that we have this beautiful building and, more important, this fine congregation of believers. As we look back at the _____ years we see God's benefits to us. Today we want to talk about these blessings and give God praise.

(Arrange beforehand to have a representative from each organization in your church tell of God's benefits in that organization and how it has affected individuals as well as the church as a whole. Include: the Sunday school superintendent, the leader of your boys' and girls' clubs, a young

48

*person from the youth group, a woman from the ladies'
group, the choir leader or a choir member, a trustee, dea-
con or deaconness, an elder, the custodian, the pastor.*

*As each one speaks of a specific blessing during the past
years, praise will arise to the Lord. It would be well to have
your choir sing several praise songs at the end of this activity. You might stand, hold hands with the persons next to
you and sing as a congregation the chorus "Alleluia" followed by "Praise the Saviour" or another praise song.)*

Looking Ahead

Speaker: Today we have been doing a great deal of remembering and reminiscing. As we have looked back we have
seen how God has led us through the years. We have
recalled specific ways that He has blessed us. We praise
Him for what He has done for us as individuals and as a
congregation.

We look back in order to learn from our mistakes. We
also look back to be encouraged by what God has done.
With Joshua we say, "Not one word of all the good words
which the Lord your God spoke concerning you has
failed" (Joshua 23:14).

We cannot, however, rest upon what has already been
done. We must go forward to fresh endeavours, greater
accomplishments, new victories. As David said to his son,
Solomon, so God says to us: "Be strong and courageous,
and act; do not fear nor be dismayed, for the Lord God,
my God, is with you. He will not fail you nor forsake you
until all the work for the service of the house of the Lord
is finished" (1 Chronicles 28:20).

Our country is suffering today because our leaders have
not been concerned enough about the future. Present
advantage has superceded long-range planning. This has
resulted in pollution, shortages, and other problems. A
course entitled "Futurism" is now being offered in many
universities and even high schools. An Encyclopedia of the
Future is being developed in Paris covering every facet of
human life.

As a church we must also plan for the future, set goals.
The board has carefully and prayerfully considered what

49

the plans for the future of our church should be. We have come up with these goals. Perhaps you have others to suggest.

(Read your list of goals. Ask someone to pray for strength to face and realize these goals. Ask someone else to offer a prayer of thanksgiving that as God has been with you in the past, so will He be in the future.)

Diamond Anniversary

Speaker: _____ marks our seventy-fifth year as an organized church. The traditional symbol for the seventy-fifth anniversary is the diamond.

The diamond is the hardest of all known substances, a mineral compound composed of carbon. Because of its hardness it is useful for cutting and grinding in industry. Because of its beauty it is used in the crowns of royalty and expensive jewelry.

A diamond is not beautiful in its original form. It must be cut, sawed, ground, and polished to bring out its beauty. After being shaped it is boiled in acid to clean it of impurities. The result is a magnificent gem.

As the diamond must go through a great deal in order to become useful and beautiful, so must the church. We have experienced God's disciplines throughout the years since first organizing as a congregation. "Those whom the Lord loves He disciplines" (Hebrews 12:6).

We have experienced difficulties and trials together with God's obvious blessings. Through it all God has been shaping us and cleansing us as the lapidary shapes and cleanses a diamond. We are all diamonds in the rough and need much cutting and polishing by the Master.

Truly "we know that God causes all things to work together for good to those who love God, to those who are called according to His purpose" (Romans 8:28). We praise Him for dealing with us in wisdom and love. We praise Him for His patience with us. We say with the psalmist: "Great is the Lord, and highly to be praised; and His greatness is unsearchable. One generation shall praise Thy

50

works to another, and shall declare Thy mighty acts"
(Psalm 145:3-4).

As we celebrate the seventy-fifth anniversary of our
church, our diamond jubilee, we declare with much gratitude to God: "Great is Thy faithfulness!" (Lamentations
3:23).

*(The facts about diamonds can also be adapted to a dia-
mond wedding anniversary celebration.)*

DECORATIONS

The principal decoration at this event should be a banner
announcing your theme. (See directions for making banners
on page 25). You may want to display a banner in the fellowship hall where you will have your refreshments as well as in
the sanctuary where you will hold your anniversary service.

Pictures of the church in its various stages of growth
should also be part of the decorating scheme for this event.
This could include ground-breaking, charter members, the
original building, additions or new buildings, and the church
members at work.

It can also include pictures of memorable events such as
Sunday school picnics, valentine banquet, a Christmas program or other festive occasions of the church. These can be
displayed in albums or, better still, mounted on posterboard
with appropriate captions and hung on the wall for all to see.

Individuals in your congregation may have small ceramic
churches that they would be willing to loan as part of the
decorating theme. These would add interest to the serving
table if you have your refreshments buffet style or to the
head table if you have a sit-down meal.

A congregation may have commemorative plates made
with the picture of their church and the dates of its existence.
These are sold to members and friends who desire a
memento of the occasion. This can serve as a fund-raising
idea for the women's group or youth group.

And remember that flowers are one of the best ways to
add color and freshness to your decorations.

Anniversary Reflections

We pause on this our special day
To think of blessings past.
And how the Lord has cared for us
From first day to the last.

Tho' few in number way back then,
The Lord was in our midst.
We got together ev'ry week
And always bro't the kids.

We asked the Lord to bless this work
He told us that He would
If true to Him we'd always be
And on His precepts stood.

He's led us thru' some waters deep
Sore trials came our way;
Sometimes we didn't understand,
But weathered thru' the fray.

Oh, many are the loyal folks
Who worked and gave and prayed;
And many are the loved ones gone
Now to their rest are laid.

Today we have an eager group
Who help the church to grow;
They brighten all the corners here
And keep the light aglow.

Yes, God was in our midst back then;
He's with us yet today.
Oh, may we faithful be to Him
And let Him lead the way.

(Betty Jo Mathis)

Moses' Anniversary Speech

Moses called the Jews together
    and said, "Now folks, please listen:
We're nearly to the promised land
    and the milk and honey glisten.
There's something I must say to you
    before you cross the waters,
So gather all together—
    all your sons and all your daughters.
Today is anniversary day
    in case you have forgot;
It was forty years ago
    we left Mount Sinai's hallowed spot,
And started on our journey
    to the promised land anew.
And the multitude, remember,
    was a mixed and motley crew:
But do you recollect," he said,
    "how God led us by His cloud,
How He fed us with the manna—
    tho' some grumbled long and loud?"
And our shoes, they never did wear out,
    our feet they never swelled;
But in spite of all His mercies,
    many doubted and rebelled.
But God had His hand upon us
    and He'd never let us go;
Now it's forty years thereafter
    and He'd have us all to know
The reason for His testing
    thru' all the weary days now past:
He just wanted us to trust Him,
    on His mercy to be cast.
He wanted us to know that man
    cannot live by earthly bread;
His holy Word is meant for food
    and by it man must be fed.
And as a father whips his son
    so God chastened now and then;
It was meant to show the folks around
    that we belonged to Him.
Oh, those years were very humbling,
    there were failures by the score;

But ev'ry time we wept in sorrow,
      God saw and saved once more.
So as we think about our past
      and the paths that we have trod;
It was not our strength and goodness
      but the love and grace of God
That led us safely thru the years
      where we look back now and say,
"He bro't us here on eagle's wings
      Oh, beware to disobey!"

(Betty Jo Mathis)

MORTGAGE BURNING CEREMONY

If possible, invite the pastor that served you when your church or addition was built to return for the mortgage burning. Have your service Sunday afternoon after a potluck dinner. This will enable friends from other churches to attend.

After appropriate musical selections and a challenge by the visiting pastor, assemble the members of the church board on the platform. As they stand in a semicircle, each one in turn will walk to the podium and read a selected verse or verses of Scripture. Some suggestions would be:

2 Chronicles 2:6
Psalm 27:4
Psalm 84:1-2, 10
Deuteronomy 4:9
Psalm 145:7
1 Chronicles 29:16
Psalm 118:1
Psalm 115:1

The chairman of the congregation or the present pastor will then bring out a facsimile of the mortgage on a metal tray (do not burn the actual papers). The visiting pastor or the treasurer of the church will light a match to it while all watch it burn.

After the mortgage papers have become ashes, the pastor
and others will lead in prayers of thanksgiving to God for
what He has done and a song of praise. The pastor then may
give a short challenge, "Where do we go from here?"
emphasizing the need to go on to further accomplishments in
the work of God's kingdom.

The following could be read as a poem or sung to the tune
of "Bless This House."[1]

Bless This Church

Bless this house of God, we pray,
    May Thy light shine every day.
Bless these walls, so firm and strong,
    Fill them with Thy praise and song.
Bless the fellowship so dear,
    May we share each joy and tear.
Bless this door that opens wide,
    Bless each one that comes inside.

Bless these windows shining bright,
    Letting in God's heavenly light.
Bless the Word that's given here,
    May its truth be ever clear.
Bless the one that You did call.
    Bless his home and loved ones all.
Bless us all that we may be,
    Fit, O Lord, to worship Thee.
Bless us all, that one day, we
    May dwell, O Lord, with Thee.

(Marilyn Johnson)

1. "Bless This House," by May H. Brahe, copyright Boosey and Co., Ltd.

3

Pastor's Welcome and Farewell

WELCOMING THE PASTOR

One of the nicest ways you can welcome your new pastor is to have his home clean and ready to move into with the cupboards full of staples and canned goods. What a joy for the pastor's wife, weary from traveling, to find necessary food in the cupboard and refrigerator so that she needn't immediately shop for groceries in order to feed her family.

It is also extremely helpful to the pastor and his family as they are getting settled in their new home when members of the congregation invite them over for the main meal of the day. Instead of inviting them for lunch, however, which would take several hours out of their workday, bring in sandwiches or a casserole so they can continue getting settled without interruption.

The first few weeks in a new church are lonely ones for the pastor's family. Ties have been broken and new friendships not yet established. It takes time for the pastor and his wife to become acquainted and to feel at home in their new congregation.

Think of ways to accomplish this quickly and without strain. Short visits by members of the church would help,

57

and, as previously mentioned, invitations for dinner or even merely for coffee after church.

Some folks feel they cannot invite the pastor and family over until they have the time and energy to prepare a fancy meal. The pastor would be just as pleased to be invited over for coffee after church. After he has preached, a pastor often feels a let-down. He is weary, and Satan is at hand to attack. How comforting it is to feel the love and acceptance of a member of the congregation who says, "How about coming over for a cup of coffee?"

Remember Peter Marshall's words: "A small deed done is better than a great deed planned."

One church to which we came had a progressive dinner (each course served at a different home) even before our official welcoming service. Everyone wore a name tag. We learned a lot of names that evening and began to know quite a number of people chatting at the various homes as the dinner progressed. It was an excellent ice-breaker.

Many churches officially welcome their pastor with a special Sunday afternoon service that includes a program.

A time of refreshments and visiting would follow.

Seat the pastor and his wife where people can come and greet them, or if they prefer, let them mingle with the crowd and get acquainted. Be sensitive to their needs; some pastors and wives are shy, believe it or not!

PROGRAMS

Our Promise

Use the following as a guideline for pledging your support to your new pastor. Read it as a congregation and then give the pastor a copy to keep in his study, or make a copy for everyone present.

We the members of _(church name)_ promise:

> that we won't expect our pastor to be an errand boy; we'll call someone else if Junior misses the bus or if Grandma Brown needs to go to the doctor.

58

that we will share the burden of visiting the sick and the hurting and not expect our pastor to do it all, knowing that this can become overwhelming when added to his many other duties.
that we will not fuss if the pastor does not come to visit us, knowing he is busy visiting the new ones and the hurting. If we want a visit from him we will invite him to dinner or over for coffee after church.

we will not expect the pastor's children to behave better than ours. We will neither criticize them nor indulge them but treat them like the other children of the congregation.

to respect the pastor's privacy. We will not call during the morning hours when he is in prayer and Bible study unless absolutely necessary. Neither will we call him on his day off but permit him and his wife to enjoy one day a week without church problems.

to remember that our pastor is human and needs encouragement and love like anyone else. He is constantly giving out to others. We will do our best to give encouragement to him, commending him for jobs well done.

knowing that our pastor needs spiritual refreshment, we will occasionally send him and his wife away for a few days, gladly paying the expenses. This may be to a spiritual retreat or merely for a time of quiet for themselves.

to be straightforward with our pastor, going to him if something is bothering us instead of talking behind his back. We will ask ourselves, "Is this really important enough to bother him with?" If it is only a trifle we'll forget it.

to pray for our pastor instead of criticizing him.

to include our pastor's family in holiday celebrations especially if they are far away from their own families.

to ask not what our pastor can do for us, but what we can do for him.

Introducing Each Other

Often members of a group introduce themselves by stating their names in turn around a circle. It is usually difficult to remember even one name. A better way is to have each per-

son introduce the one on his right by saying something perti-
nent about him that begins with the initials of his name, such
as: "This is Alice Paulson—she's always perky;" or, "This is
Bill Ingram, big imagination."

Or if you prefer, forget the initials and simply tell something interesting about the person on your right. For
instance, "Don works at the bank, but he does furniture
upholstery on the side;" or, "Jane teaches piano and does
volunteer work at the hospital."

Picture Gallery

You could make your pastor and family feel at home at
their welcoming party if they could see their own faces on
the walls of your fellowship hall. Sharp black-and-white
snapshots can be enlarged many times to make charming
picture-posters. Contact the church from which your pastor
is coming for snapshots that you can have blown up in this
way. Display at the welcoming service. If possible, obtain
some amusing pictures as well. A good laugh will benefit
everyone.

Getting Acquainted

If you do not have a pictorial church directory, it would be
a good idea to make one just for your new pastor and his
family. Ask for snapshots from each family with a description
of the work, interests, hobbies, and gifts of the members.
Paste in a scrapbook and present to the pastor at his welcoming ceremony. This will be a great help in acquainting him
and his family with the church members.

Inevitable Change

Speaker: We all agree that our world is changing. Although
probably none of you here can remember the horse and
buggy days, perhaps a few of you can remember when
television and spaceships were only dreams. Scientists
predict unbelievable changes in the future, such as food
produced by microbiological engineering instead of farm-
ing and self-contained colonies in space.

Changes are occurring in the English language. A few years ago such expressions as zip code, tax shelter, lifestyle, hangup, uptight, putdown, and copout were unknown. Americans are also changing in size. Today's male college student weighs in ten pounds heavier than his father and is one inch taller, while a girl exceeds her mother by two pounds and one-half inch. The size of American feet are changing, too, according to the shoe manufacturers, and even the size of seats in public buildings to accomodate growing posteriors.

Society is also changing. What was considered immoral a few years ago has become acceptable behavior in many circles.

Change makes us feel uncomfortable. We cling to the familiar, what we know. When we must exchange it for the unknown, stress develops.

Today we are celebrating a change—a new pastor. Pastor _____, we realize that this is a stressful time for you and your family. You will have to adjust to a different church, a new board, a new city, a different house, new neighbors. Your children will have to attend a new school and make new friends. We hope we can make this time of adjustment pleasant for you through our love and understanding. Please let us know if there is any way to help you make it easier.

We as a congregation must also make an adjustment— to a new pastor and family. We are happy that you are here to minister to us and work with us in spreading the gospel. We believe this change is going to benefit us all and bring glory to the Lord. We will try not to compare you with the pastors that have gone before, and we hope you will not continually say, "In my last church we did it *this* way." We hope that we can give a little and that you can give a little to make this transition easier. We trust that we as a congregation will be open to new ideas and not insist, "But we've never done it that way before!" We must not resist change when it is for our good.

Although the world about us is changing, sometimes almost too quickly for us to keep up, there are some things that never change.

God does not. "For I the Lord, do not change; therefore you, O sons of Jacob, are not consumed" (Malachi 3:6). "Jesus Christ is the same yesterday and today, yes and forever" (Hebrews 13:8).

Neither does God's Word change. "Forever, O Lord, Thy word is settled in heaven" (Psalm 119:89). Jesus said: "Heaven and earth will pass away, but My words shall not pass away" (Matthew 24:35).

With an unchangeable God and His unchangeable Word as our focus, we face this change in our church with glad and expectant hearts and pray that you and your family will as well. As the songwriter of "Be Still My Soul" put it: "In every change, He faithful will remain."

We are glad you changed churches. Thank you for coming, and may God bless us all as we serve Him together at _(name of church)_ .

Skit: What the Pastor Should Be

Characters: Emma, Olga, Henrietta (three elderly women)
                   Don, Ed, Bill (three middle-aged men)
                   Steve, Sandy, Trent (three young people)
(The three elderly women sit in chairs to the left in a little huddle.)

Emma: I hear we're in the market for a new pastor.

Olga: Yes, poor Pastor Ulrich didn't last long, did he?

Henrietta: *(shakes head)* He sure didn't, but then I didn't really expect him to. He had such big ideas.

Olga: *(nodding)* All he ever thought about was making the church grow. That bothered me.

Emma: Me, too. I'd say it's big enough. What's wrong with a small cozy church?

Henrietta: If it gets any bigger we old 'uns will really get left out. Pastor Ulrich hardly had time to visit us the way it was.

Emma: Oh, he visited me once in a while, but he was always in such a hurry. As soon as I started telling him about when my family came over from Norway—you know my parents had eight children and Maria got the whooping cough on the ship over, and the baby nearly died, and my grandma was along, and she was all crippled up with rheumatism, and my mother was dreadfully seasick, and—

Olga: I thought we were talking about the pastor.

Emma: I know. Whenever I started telling him about my family I'd be only half through and he'd suddenly suggest we have a word of prayer because it was time for him to go. *(Sigh)* I never did get my story finished clear to the end.

Olga: He impressed me that way, too. Always in a hurry.

Henrietta: Not much time for us old folks.

Emma: I sure hope the new one that comes will have tea with me often and spend the afternoon without rushing off in the middle of my stories.

Olga: Say, I just thought of something. There's a man coming to candidate next Sunday. Why don't we kind of put a bug in his ear as to what we expect in a pastor.

Henrietta: Good idea. Why don't I be the spokesman for the three of us!

(They stand up.)

Emma: Pastor Ulrich would have said "spokes*person*."

(They begin to leave.)

Olga: That's another thing—he smacked of women's lib. If there's anything I can't stand—

(Three men enter and walk about the stage as they talk.)

Bill: The way I look at it, we've got to have a pastor with organizational ability, someone to make this church grow. We need to push out the back wall, enlarge the sanctuary.

Don: What for? The church is only half full now.

Bill: That's what I mean—we've got to fill this place. We've got to get a pastor who will bring in the people.

Ed: You mean someone who is good in the pulpit?

Bill: Well, yes, and one who has administrative ability, someone who can get this church moving.

Don: I think we need a man who does a lot of visitation. When I was a kid our pastor visited every home in the congregation once a week.

Ed: How many families did you have in your church?

Don: Well, only about ten, come to think of it. And we couldn't pay him much, so he usually came at mealtime.

He always showed up Saturday afternoons at our house—late afternoon.

Ed: As far as I'm concerned we pay our pastor to preach, not visit. He should be in that church study at *least* three hours a day, maybe more. Otherwise he won't be able to feed us, let alone pray for us.

Bill: Of course that's true, but we can't forget the organizational end. Our pastor should attend ministerial meetings, know what's going on in the community, take his stand against things, get in the fight against evil.

Ed: But he must be a godly man, not one of these liberals that flirt with the world. He's got to keep these new-fangled things out of the church like that horrible rock and roll music.

Bill: Oh, we'd never let that in, but gospel music with a Western flavor, that's different. I go for that.

Ed: Cowboy music in the church? *(looks up and rolls his eyes)* I hope our new pastor won't approve of that!
(They begin to move off the stage.)

Bill: I'll mention these things to the man coming to candidate on Sunday.
(Three young people enter. Steve carries a guitar and sprawls on a chair. Sandy is eating a bag of popcorn. She sits cross-legged on the floor. Trent stands hugging his basketball, occasionally dribbling it.)

Steve: *(picks on his guitar)* A new pastor! I hope we get a young one for a change.

Sandy: Well, Pastor Ulrich wasn't really old—he was forty.

Steve: I mean *young* young like us, without those mothball ideas.

Sandy: Someone that's really with it *(jumps up, snaps her fingers and twirls around, spilling some of her popcorn).*

Trent: I'd go for a pastor who'd play basketball with us.

Steve: Yeah, and take us skiing.

Sandy: And swimming.

Trent: And to retreats—things like that.

Steve: I sure hope we'll get one that will change the music around here. That dead stuff we sing on Sunday morning— *(shakes head)* Reminds me of a funeral.

Sandy: *(snaps her fingers and does a little jig)* I know what you mean. Something swinging for a change to liven things up around here. I play the drums at school. Why not at church?

Trent: Maybe we should talk to this guy who's coming to candidate on Sunday, just let him know how we feel about things. Steve, you're good with words. Why don't you do the talking, and we'll back you up?

Steve: *(strums his guitar a few seconds)* OK, will do. We've got to throw our weight around to change things in our church.

(Youths saunter off, strumming the guitar, eating popcorn, and dribbling the ball.)

(The nine characters enter, the elderly women in a group at the left, the men in the center, and the youth to the right.)

Bill: *(looking at a letter)* I can't understand it. This is the fourth pastor that has turned us down.

Steve: *(to Trent and Sandy)* Oh, well, they're all probably old fogies anyway.

Don: Where is their sense of dedication?

Emma: (shakes head) Men of the cloth are certainly not what they used to be!

(All exit)

(After the skit one of the characters or another speaker could step forward and add the following:)

Speaker: This skit has perhaps exaggerated the way we think and feel about our pastors. It makes us aware that we all have different desires and expectations of him as well as different needs we hope he will fulfill. No man is capable of meeting all those desires, expectations, and needs. No man has all the gifts. *(Read Romans 12:5-8 and 1 Corinthians 12:4-11.)* God has given His church all the necessary gifts to accomplish His will on earth. Each of us has a contribution to make, not only the pastor.

We thank God for the gifts of our pastor, but we realize he is a human being like ourselves and we cannot expect him to be superhuman. Pastor _____, we pledge ourselves to stand with you and fill up any lacks you may have with the gifts God has given us as lay people in His church. We will pray for you, be loyal to you, and love you

65

as long as you are our shepherd. We don't expect perfection from you and hope you will not expect it from us either. Together we will look to the Lord, for our expectation is from Him.

God bless you as you begin your ministry among us.

DECORATIONS

A large banner saying "Welcome" would probably be the best decoration you could have for this event. Fresh flowers or plants would add to the festive atmosphere.

If possible, obtain a picture of your pastor and his family and display in a conspicuous place in your fellowship hall. Draw attention to the picture with another "Welcome" sign complete with colorful crepe paper streamers. Perhaps your new pastor's wife could be persuaded to lend you some snapshots of your new pastor. Even a baby picture or pictures from his childhood and teen years would be fun. Make a display of them with appropriate captions. Include some of the pastor's wife and family as well. This will be another way for you to get to know your new pastor.

POEMS

He Leads Me by Green Pastors

Lord, bless the pastors green and new
    who hardly know the score,
Who'd take Thy sacred Sword in hand
    and sally forth to war.

With commentary on the shelf
    and Bible in the hand,
Lord bless those zealous pulpiteers
    who'd join the prophet's band.

May many vict'ries be their lot,
    their slain Egyptians few;
As they would brave the battle's heat
    a soldier, Lord, for You.

May they be satisfied, dear Lord,
　　to simply sow the seed
And leave the tally up to You,
　　Who knows both heart and deed.

O keep them, Lord, so occupied
　　with washing dear saints' feet
That they've no time for splitting hairs,
　　no time for scorner's seat.

O lay Thy hand upon the heads
　　of those You've truly called
And keep it there thru' all the years,
　　as heads turn gray and bald.

Tho' weak may die upon the way
　　and cowards never start,
Lord, give Your pastors, green and new,
　　a tough but tender heart.

(Betty Jo Mathis)

New Preacher

We've got a new preacher down at the church.
The pulpit committee has finished its search.
The ladies have scrubbed—the parsonage painted.
Social committee will soon get acquainted.

The preacher's unloading his stuff at the manse;
He's dressed in a sweatshirt and faded old pants.
The neighbors are watching, their tongues in their cheeks;
How long will this one stay? Years? Months? Mebbe weeks??

The Church Board is nervous—wonders how it will go.
And all the parish'ners are anxious to know:
Is he quiet? loud? pound the pulpit? or shout?
Or a meek little man—no power, no clout?

The young folks are wondering: how old are his kids?
Will friendly they be and fit right in our midst?
The women are hoping his wife is a pearl;
Not flashy, not dowdy, just a down home girl.

67

The preacher's praying as he hauls in more books,
"Help me love 'em, dear Lord, in spite of their looks!"
His wife smooths her hair as she looks at the mess,
"Will the women accept me? How should I dress?"

The girls bite their nails, "Will we have any friends?"
The boys hunt for a place to build rabbit pens.
The baby is squalling—he's hungry and wet.
His bottle is empty—his crackers are et.

But then up the walk comes a happy-faced bunch,
With warm friendly smiles, and they're bringing a lunch!
Doubts melt away as they give handshakes and hugs,
Start carrying boxes and laying down rugs.

Soon tensions are gone, the fears all subside
As they talk and they laugh and work side by side.
Each knows that this venture will be a success
If together they work and trust God to bless;

If each is aware of his own special place
And daily spends time at the throne of God's grace.

(Betty Jo Mathis)

Life in a Fishbowl

The small town preacher, God bless his soul
    Lives his life in a public fish bowl.
There on the corner of First and Main
    The manse is where we can see it plain.

We know when his kids have angry fights
    When his dog has pups, or barks or bites.
We can see the folks who come and go
    And wonder if they be friend or foe.

No secrets can hide behind his doors
    Nor skeleton lurk beneath his floors.
The preacher's life, like an open book
    Is revealed for all to take a look.

We can tell when things are tight and tense,
    And we trust the Lord will give us sense
To sympathize with the preacher's woes
    And help him face life's bitter blows.

For tho' he's a man with sacred trust,
    The preacher is also made from dust.
He laughs and cries, gets wet when it rains,
    Has headaches, heartaches, stresses and strains.

City preachers get lost in the mob
    But small town men who are on the job
Belong to the flock, they're not their own
    Nor are days or night, flesh nor bone.

Lord, bless the preachers who live in fish bowls
    Give them vict'ry in battling for souls;
Help your children, both preachers and flocks,
    To think before they throw any rocks.

(Betty Jo Mathis)[1]

A Word to the Wives

If you, like me, are a preacher's wife
(A blessed privilege—a busy life)
A part of your duty, you will find,
Is to speak these words from time to time—
When hubby's depressed, ready to screech,
"My dear, you must practice what you preach."

When folks don't listen nor change their life,
'Tis then that the preacher needs a wife
To prod him along, lest faith grows small,
"Keep on, dear, don't throw in the towel—
It will take a while, their hearts to reach,
Meantime, you must practice what you preach."

He's preached on joy and he's preached on trust.
He's preached on faith for all of the just.
But his smile of joy has all but fled

1. From *Dinner of Herbs*, by Betty Jo Mathis. Used by permission.

And worry now lines his brow instead.
It is then we wives must still beseech,
"Take heart and practice what you preach."

Words fitly spoke—like apples of gold,
Spoken before a warm heart grows cold,
Spoken when lures of this earth creep near,
Spoken to him when none else can hear.
"Dear, you're beyond the enemy's reach—
Stand firm and practice what you preach."

Brag on his sermons, nor dwell on faults.
Pray for him much when Satan assaults.
Speak of mistakes in tones hushed and sweet.
Tell him you're glad to be his help-meet.
Be faithful, kind, as God's Word teaches,
Help him to practice what he preaches.

(Betty Jo Mathis)[2]

The Preacher's Wife

You may think it quite an easy task
    And just a pleasant life;
But it really takes a lot of grace
    To be a preacher's wife.

She's supposed to be a paragon,
    Without a fault in view;
A saint when in the parsonage,
    As well as in the pew.

Her home must be a small hotel
    For folks that chance to roam,
And yet have peace and harmony—
    The perfect preacher's home.

Whenever groups are called to meet,
    Her presence must be there;
And yet the members all agree
    She should live a life of prayer.

2. From *Of Throne and Footstool,* by Betty Jo Mathis. Used by permission.

Though hearing people's burdens,
    Their griefs both night and day,
She's supposed to spread but sunshine
    To those along the way.

She must lend a sympathetic ear
    To every tale of woe,
And then forget about it,
    Lest it to others go.

Her children must be models rare
    Of sweetness and poise,
But still stay on the level
    With other girls and boys.

You may think it quite an easy task
    And just a pleasant life,
But it really takes a lot of grace
    To be a preacher's wife.

(Author Unknown)

FAREWELLING THE PASTOR

DO'S AND DON'TS

Don't:

make your pastor feel guilty for leaving

make his last weeks difficult by insisting he and his family come for a meal even if it must be breakfast because his schedule is so full.

say, "If there's anything I can do for you, let me know." He won't.

delay his leaving with last-minute picture taking, and so on

leave him out of things just because he won't be around much longer.

71

Do:

invite him for a farewell meal at your home before the last two weeks when he is swamped with invitations.

plan the farewell service before the strain of last-minute packing.

keep the farewell service upbeat and cheerful without making it a celebration.

offer to take the children when the pastor and his wife are packing.

offer to do time-consuming tasks such as cleaning the oven and the cupboards for them after they have left.

provide a place for them to stay overnight the last night or two after their beds are in the moving van.

send along a tasty lunch of sandwiches and fruit if they are traveling by car.

send along small gifts for the children to open along the way to keep them amused: crayons, coloring books, small games, gum, and so forth.

give them your blessing without acting relieved that they are leaving.

promise to pray for them if you really mean it.

PROGRAMS

Official Farewell

There are several possible ways to say farewell to your pastor. You might gather for an informal get-together at the church and give people opportunity to tell what the pastor's ministry has meant to them and to wish him well in his future ministry. Include humorous anecdotes from the past years so the occasion will not be unduly solemn but joyous.

Ask the pastor to tell you about where he is going and what his plans are.

Sing the pastor's favorite hymn and decorate the fellowship hall with his favorite color. For refreshments serve his favorite food if possible.

Or simply have an open house without a structured program where people can come to greet the pastor and his family, have some refreshments, and leave to make room for others.

If you wish to give gifts, money is most appropriate. A move always entails extra expenses, and few pastors are overpaid. A plate can be passed, and donors simply sign their name to a card. Or individuals can give cards with their money gifts. A money tree is a good idea.

Make a Scrapbook

When your pastor is preparing to leave make up a scrapbook for him and his family. Ask each church family to contribute a picture (snapshots will do) and a few words of farewell. Some will no doubt want to include a letter telling of what the pastor's ministry has meant to them. This makes a lovely memento for the pastor to keep and cherish. You might also include newspaper clippings of various significant church events and pictures of members who have passed away during his ministry.

This Is Your Life

Obtain information from the pastor's wife about his boyhood and youthful days, including pranks if possible. Write up a story to be read at the farewell, or acted out, telling or showing as many personal anecdotes as you can come up with that highlight his life and ministry.

If you have slides, show them and comment on them. Or have old black-and-white snapshots of the pastor and his family blown up and put around the fellowship hall.

End this farewell service with testimonies from people of a variety of ages who would like to share what the pastor's ministry has meant to them and wish him well in his future ministry.

73

Pantomime

Have a group of young people pantomime various events in the pastor's life and the life of the church during the years he has been with them. This could include a new baby, building an addition to the church, a sporting event, a memorable Sunday school picnic, the day he got a ticket for speeding, the day he forgot the wedding he was to perform, or any other special event.

The pastor should have first chance to guess what the pantomime signifies. If he cannot guess, other members of the congregation may try.

Give a prize to the one who guesses the most correctly.

Hats Off to You!

Have your pastor and wife lead a varied and interesting life? You may enjoy focusing on the various "hats" they've worn through the years.

Snoop around and use real hats that were meaningful to them, if possible. For instance, did they meet at college? Find a "beanie" from their college initiation days. Did they work at a fast food place? Can you borrow a cap from there or make a replica of it? Were either or both in the military? Focus on these hats too.

Note jobs, hobbies, interests—actual hats worn and figurative ones. A mother, for example, figuratively wears the hat of a nurse, teacher, baker, taxi driver, and psychologist among other professions.

Select individuals who will model these hats while they (or you) tell about the period of life in which that hat was important to the couple.

Make this a humorous time but one that does not poke fun at or embarrass anyone.

Conclude the comments by saying, "Our hats are off to you for the good job you've done as our pastor and wife."

Changes

(Using the material in "Inevitable Change" on page 60 talk about the changes that have occurred since your pastor has

74

been with you: babies born into the congregation, baptisms, graduations, weddings, funerals, new converts, new members, changes in church facilities, growth, and so on.)

Speaker: We thank you for being our faithful shepherd through all of these changes. You are a part of us and our families. It is hard to see you leave. We realize, however, that God is leading you in this change, and we would not stand in your way. We will pray for you as you go to unfamiliar surroundings and people who are strangers to you. We will pray that the change will not prove too stressful to you or your family but that you will make a quick adjustment.

Pray also for us that we will adjust to our new pastor and his family. May we, in turn, make their adjustment go smoothly.

We send you to your new place of service with these words from Joshua 1:9: "Have I not commanded you? Be strong and courageous! Do not tremble or be dismayed, for the Lord your God is with you wherever you go."

Pastor Appreciation

We all realize that pastors sometimes get discouraged and need a special boost from their congregations to assure them they are appreciated and loved. Surprise your pastor with an appreciation Sunday. After the customary church announcements, have one of the church officers come forward and give a little talk of appreciation. Hand out cards to the congregation on which these words are typed: "I appreciate Pastor _____ because" and leave a space in which the recipient can write what he likes about the pastor.

Collect the cards after the service and present to the pastor in a basket tied with a bow. You may want to do this at an evening service and serve refreshments in his honor, or you may want to do it at a Sunday morning service and serve a potluck dinner afterwards. Or you may not want to serve food at all but simply let your pastor go home to read the comments and be encouraged by them.

DECORATIONS

Avoid making this a gala occasion by over-decorating. Your pastor may think you are glad he is leaving! A banner stating, "Farewell, Pastor _____" or "Thank You, Pastor _____" would be appropriate.

Put up a money tree in the fellowship hall (directions on p. 31) where friends can give their pastor a farewell gift or use the wishing well idea. Give the pastor a boutonniere and his wife a fresh flower corsage to wear for the occasion.

POEMS

Farewell, Pastor

It seems as if you came only yesterday,
    And now they are telling us that you will go away.
Is it really _____ years that you have served us here?
    Oh, how quickly time has flown, and you have grown so
    dear.

Your duties have been many: teaching, visiting, too,
    Counseling the troubled who don't know what to do.
Sometimes preaching hard to us when we have gone astray,
    Praying that we'll all come back to the narrow way.

You've baptized and you've married, confirmed and dedicated.
    You've watched our children grow from babes until they
    graduated.
You've preached the funeral sermons of our loved ones who
    have gone.
    You've helped us put them in the grave 'til resurrection's
    dawn.

You've wept with us in sorrow, rejoiced when we were glad.
    You've brought us words of comfort when we were feeling
    sad.
You've taught us what the Bible says, and how we need to
    live,
    To be obedient to the Lord, to love and to forgive.

76

We thank you, Pastor _____ for all you've done for us.
  Forgive us for the times that we have balked and made a
    fuss.
We really love you dearly, and though we now must part,
  We'll always keep a part of you right here within our heart.

(Matilda Nordtvedt)

You're Leaving Something Behind!

Dear Pastor friend, the time has come when you'll be moving on.
The Lord has called to other fields and you will soon be gone.
You've packed your books, your notes, your maps; you've sorted
    thru' your files.
You've cleaned out all your desk drawers, got rid of stuff by piles.
You have checked in every corner to see if all was packed
But everything's accounted for—it's all been neatly stacked.
But there is something you've not boxed—it's simply slipped your
    mind.
You're not aware you're leaving it, but 'twill be left behind.
It's not a book beneath a chest nor a sock behind a door;
It's not a thing we'll mail to you—you've left it times before.
You have a strange forgetful way of stringing out a trail,
But no one will rebuke you and none will ever say you've failed.
For the thing that you will never pack, the thing you'll leave behind
Is your inspiration to us here—your influence, rare and kind.
We're glad you're leaving it with us—that it's not in your stacks;
Because we need it in our lives—we're glad you've left your tracks!

(Betty Jo Mathis)

77

4

Graduation

Many parents have an open house in their homes for their graduates, allowing friends and relatives to come with their congratulations and gifts and enjoy refreshments and a time of visiting.

Over and above this, the church does well to honor their graduates with a special service for them. If the graduates have musical talents, use them in the program. Do one of the skits on "God's Will" or give the "Graduation Promises." Introduce each one and let them share their plans for the coming fall. Pray for each one by name.

Have a time of refreshments after the service. A large sheet cake with the words "Congratulations, Graduates" or "God Bless You, Graduates" would be appropriate.

PROGRAMS

Graduation Promises

Think of an interesting way to give these promises to your graduates. You may want to type them on slips of paper, fold, and put in a basket. Each graduate could choose one to read aloud.

I will instruct you and teach you in the way which you should go; I will counsel you with my eye upon you. (Psalm 32:8)

How precious also are Thy thoughts to me, O God! How vast is the sum of them: If I should count them, they would outnumber the sand. (Psalm 139:17-18)

For I know the plans that I have for you, declares the Lord, plans for welfare and not for calamity to give you a future and a hope. (Jeremiah 29:11)

Trust in the Lord with all your heart, and do not lean on your own understanding. In all your ways acknowledge Him, and He will make your paths straight. (Proverbs 3:5-6)

How blessed is the man who finds wisdom, and the man who gains understanding. For its profit is better than the profit of silver, and its gain than fine gold. (Proverbs 3:13-14)

Trust in the Lord and do good; dwell in the land and cultivate faithfulness. (Psalm 37:3)

Delight yourself in the Lord; and He will give you the desires of your heart. (Psalm 37:4)

Commit your way to the Lord, trust also in Him, and He will do it. (Psalm 37:5)

Skit: Good, Acceptable, Perfect

Characters: Mortimer, Horacio, Marie (three young people)
(Mortimer and Horacio enter.)

Mortimer: Did you get the message?
Horacio: Yes, the King asked us to come here to the palace.
Mortimer: I wonder what He wants.
Horacio: I'm sure I don't know, but I have a feeling it'll be something good.
Mortimer: What makes you say that?
Horacio: He's been so good to us already. Don't forget, Mortimer, we were His enemies at one time.
Mortimer: How could I forget? I was the greatest rebel of all—condemned to die, but He gave me a pardon.

80

Horacio: He gave me a pardon, too, but the most astounding thing of all is that He adopted us into His own family as His sons.

Mortimer: *(shakes his head)* It is almost unbelievable. To think that we, His former enemies, are part of the royal family and heirs to all the King's fortunes!

(Marie enters with two packages. On each is written in large letters "MY WILL: GOOD, ACCEPTABLE, PERFECT." She puts them on the table.)

Marie: The King asked me to give you each a gift from Him.

Horacio: *(reads)* "MY WILL: GOOD, ACCEPTABLE, PER-FECT." What does that mean?

Marie: It means that the King is offering you His good, acceptable, and perfect plan for your life.

Mortimer: How exciting! I wonder what His plan is for me! *(He reaches for the package with his name on it.)*

Marie: Wait a minute. You cannot have the package unless you are willing to follow the directions you will find inside.

Mortimer: B-but let me see what's inside. Then I'll decide if I want it or not.

Marie: *(shakes her head)* I'm sorry. The King reveals His will only to those who are willing to follow it.
(Marie sits down)

Mortimer: What shall we do? I'd like to take the gift, but not on those terms.

Horacio: Can't you trust the King, my brother? He has become our father. Think of what He has already done for us.

Mortimer: *(paces about)* I know, but I have some plans of my own. There's Louise, for instance. I have my heart set on marrying her. What if she is not in the King's plan for my life?

Horacio: Then you would be better off without her.

Mortimer: Never! I can't bear to think of such a thing! And what if I don't like what He asks me to do?

Horacio: It says His will is good, acceptable, and perfect.

Mortimer: No, I can't do it. It's too risky. You go ahead if you want to.

(Horacio reaches for his gift and opens the box to reveal a second wrapped box. There is a message on top of the box

which Horacio reads aloud.)

Horacio: "You are to enroll at the College of the Knights for training to do My service."

(Horacio starts to unwrap the second box)

Marie: *(jumps up)* No, no! You have the directions for the first step you are to take. That is enough. When you are ready for the next step you can open the next box.

Horacio: I see. It is enough to know His will for now. Oh, Mortimer, I am so happy. I am excited. The King has trusted me with His perfect will! Why don't you too accept your gift?

Mortimer: *(shakes head)* In one way I want to, but I'm afraid of what it might involve.

Horacio: I must go to thank the King.

Mortimer: Thank Him for me, too, and offer Him my apologies for declining the gift. I hope He will understand my dilemma.

(Boys leave with Marie.)

(Marie returns with a sign: TWENTY YEARS LATER.)

(Mortimer and Horacio come in different doors, clasp hands.)

Horacio: How good it is to see you!

Mortimer: And to see you!

Horacio: It has been twenty long years. Tell me, brother, how has it gone for you?

Mortimer: *(shakes head)* I have acquired much riches but very little satisfaction. Our home has been full of misery. Louise finally left me, and I'm afraid our two children are damaged beyond repair.

Horacio: Beyond repair?

Mortimer: Yes, Nathan is in prison for killing a man. *(hangs his head)*

Horacio: *(grasps his arm)* Oh, no!

Mortimer: Yes, it is true.

Horacio: And your daughter?

Mortimer: She married one of the King's enemies.

(They stand silent for a moment.)

Mortimer: How about you? What has your life been like?

Horacio: It has not been without its difficulties. As you know, the King gave me a lovely wife, Harriet. She also accepted the King's will. It has not been an easy life, but one full of meaning and challenge. We have not become wealthy with earthly possessions, but we possess great spiritual gain and contentment. We have our inheritance awaiting us as well. Yes, we found the King's will to be good, acceptable, and perfect, just as He promised.

Mortimer: *(shakes head)* I didn't believe the King's word. I thought I knew better than He. How foolish I was! What a mess I have made of my life!

Horacio: Do not despair, Mortimer. The King is gracious and willing to forgive. Perhaps He can yet make something beautiful of the years you have left.

Horacio: Do you think so? Will you go with me to ask Him?

Mortimer: Certainly. Let's go at once!

(They exit.)

Skit: God's Will for Your Life

Characters: Moderator
                Jonah
                Psalmist
                Israelite
                George Mueller

(Use puppets or real people. Put a name sign on the puppet or person to identify him.)

Moderator: Our sincere desire for you graduates is that you will find God's will for your lives. Paul calls God's will "good, acceptable, and perfect" (Romans 12:2). We can't improve on that. God's will is actually a wonderful gift that you are privileged to receive. Man's fallen nature, however, makes him want his own will instead of God's. Satan convinces him that he knows better than his Creator.

     Let us hear some testimonies from the past.

(Jonah appears.)

Jonah: Hi, I'm Jonah. Remember me? I'm the guy who had a free ride in a fish. Sounds like fun, but it wasn't. I shudder every time I think of it.

Moderator: Why don't you tell us how you got into such a predicament.

Jonah: Through disobedience to the will of God. I didn't want to go to Nineveh to preach as God commanded me. I ran in the opposite direction.

Moderator: And ended up in a fish.

Jonah: Right. It was horrible.

Moderator: What did you do?

Jonah: I prayed—confessed my sin of disobedience to the Lord. God made the fish spit me out. Was that ever a relief! You can be sure I made tracks for Nineveh after that!

Moderator: Do you have any particular message for these graduates?

Jonah: I certainly do. My advice is—don't be like me. Do what God says the first time around. If you don't, you'll have to learn the hard way as I did.

Moderator: Thanks, Jonah.

(Israelite appears.)

Moderator: Here's one of the Israelites from the Old Testament times. What do you have to say about God's will?

Israelite: I lived in the land of Judah during Jeremiah's day. Our nation was conquered by the Babylonians. They took many people captive to Babylon, but a few of us were left.

Moderator: Were you glad about that?

Israelite: Truthfully, we were frightened. The king of Babylon put a Babylonian officer over us, and one of our men killed him. We were sure we'd be in big trouble.

Moderator: What did you do?

Israelite: We asked the prophet Jeremiah to pray to God for us and ask Him to tell us what to do. We promised that we would do whatever God told us through Jeremiah, whether it was pleasant or unpleasant.

Moderator: Did you?

Israelite: No, I'm sorry to say we didn't do what Jeremiah told us. We wanted to move to *Egypt*—it seemed so much safer—but Jeremiah said God wanted us to stay right where we were in Judah, and God would take care of us. Since we didn't want to do that, we accused Jeremiah of telling us lies.

Moderator: Were you really sincere when you said you wanted to do God's will?

Israelite: I'm afraid not. We only wanted God's approval of

84

our own will. When we didn't get it we just went ahead and did what we wanted to.

Moderator: How did it turn out?

Israelite: Just as the prophet warned us it would. War and famine followed us to Egypt. There were very few survivors.

Moderator: What would be your message to these graduates?

Israelite: Don't ask God to show you His will unless you really intend to do it. Don't make up your mind what you're going to do and then ask God's approval of it. Ask Him first, and do what He directs.

Moderator: Thank you, that was very helpful. Why, here comes the psalmist!

(Psalmist enters.)

Moderator: What do you have to say about the will of God?

Psalmist: I wrote prophetically Christ's words: "I delight to do Thy will, O my God" (Psalm 40:8). Christ performed the will of His Father perfectly. I have not always done this, but I too delight in His will.

Moderator: What is the best way to know and do God's will?

Psalmist: The best way is to meditate upon God's Word. Meditation upon God's Word makes us like a tree planted by the river. It prospers. So will we. Through meditation upon God's Word we receive knowledge, counsel, wisdom. God guides us into His will as we read and meditate upon His Word and claim His precious promises as our own.

Moderator: So that is your advice to the graduates?

Psalmist: Yes, spend time in God's Word.

(George Mueller appears.)

Moderator: Why here is George Mueller. You're the man who started those orphanages in England many years ago. I suppose you know something about God's will.

George Mueller: Indeed I do. When I was young I had some mistaken notions about it, though. As a new Christian I wondered if I should apply to a certain mission society. I decided that I would decide it by the lottery. If I won the prize that would mean it was God's will to apply. I won and applied to the missionary society only to be turned down. That showed me that casting lots or drawing straws was not the way to determine God's will.

Moderator: What is the way?

George Mueller: Waiting upon God. I learned to trust God as I cared for hundreds of orphans. He never failed me. He always supplied our needs in the nick of time. I began to look at obstacles with pleasure rather than with anxiety, a new opportunity for God to show what He could do.

Moderator: Can you give us an example of this?

George Mueller: Yes. At one time in my life I felt led to take a prolonged trip to Germany for the purpose of strengthening the Christians there and also publishing my life story in German. Five obstacles stood in the way: three were regarding finances and two were regarding personnel to take my place at the orphanage during my absence.

Moderator: Did these obstacles discourage you?

George Mueller: No, I had a secret satisfaction in the greatness of the difficulties that were in the way. So far from being cast down on account of them, they delighted my soul; for I only desired to do the will of the Lord in this matter.

Moderator: Did God remove the obstacles?

George Mueller: Yes, but not right away. After about six or seven weeks of praying and waiting, God opened the way for me.

Moderator: What advice would you give these graduates?

George Mueller: Don't get into a stew if a door doesn't open for you at once. Keep praying and waiting for God. Rest in Him—He will bring His will to pass in your life.

Moderator: Thank you, George Mueller, and the rest of you friends for your contributions. We have learned from Jonah about the folly of running away from God's will. We have learned from the Israelite about the mistake of doing God's will only if it coincides with our will. We have heard from the psalmist about the importance of learning God's will from His Word. George Mueller taught us the necessity of waiting on God in trust and confidence to work out His will for us.

For you graduates we pray with Paul "that you may be filled with the knowledge of His will in all spiritual wisdom and understanding, so that you may walk in a manner worthy of the Lord, to please Him in all respects, bearing fruit in every good work and increasing in the knowledge of God" (Col. 1:9-10).

God bless each one of you! We will be praying for you!

DECORATIONS

Inexpensive small graduate dolls can be purchased at a hobby store to decorate the cake or the tables. Or dress up a girl and boy doll as graduates for the serving table. Also use catalogs of various colleges as part of the decor.

If possible, display the graduation pictures of the graduates you are honoring. Arrange on a wall or set on a table. Return them to the graduates after the event.

Make a banner (see p. 25) with the words "Congratulations!" "We're Proud of You!" or "God Bless You!"

Mortarboard Nutcups

Make graduation caps out of black construction paper for nutcups.

For individual mortarboards: Cut construction paper in 3-inch squares and strips 7 1/2 inches in length and 2 inches wide, one square and one strip for each hat.

To make tassels, cut three strands of embroidery thread each 9 inches long in different colors and one strand 6 inches long. Hold the three strands together, fold in half and tie at the middle of the fold with the 6-inch strand. Braid the 3 strands (6 threads, after folding) and one end of the 6-inch strand together for about 1 inch. Tie a knot in the braid and let the remainder of the strands hang free.

For ease in assembly:

1) To attach the tassels to the squares, poke the single thread that is left from the 6-inch strand through a hole in the center of the square top. Tape the strand on the underside of the square to secure the tassel.

2) Lay squares with tassel side down.

3) Clip along one edge of the 7 1/2-inch strip at 1/2 inch

intervals, cutting in about 1/2 inch from the edge. Curve the strip into a ring and glue or tape the 2-inch ends together to form a brim.

4) Fold the tabs you have cut into the center of the ring and dab clear-drying glue on the bottom of each.

5) Fasten the tabs to the underside of the square, holding until the glue bonds.

6) Set the cap down over small filled nutcups about 1 1/2 inches in diameter.

POEMS

Commencement Reflections

I'm standing here with this gown
    dangling 'round my knees
And this mortarboard upon my head—
    what if I should sneeze?
I feel a little foolish
    and the other guys do too,
But we joke and laugh and scuffle
    like cool guys always do.

The band will soon be playing
    and the solemn march will start;
But in spite of all the trappin's,
    there's a battle in my heart.
The gym is quickly filling
    with uncles, aunts and cousins;
There are puzzled little kids
    and babies by the dozens.

Mom and Dad are way up front
    and even Granddad came!
Oh, Granddad wouldn't miss,
    altho' he's getting awful lame.
I can see my sister, proud—
    little brother's toothless grin.
Each teacher soon will take his place—
    the speeches will begin.

And when they call my name at last,
    my feet will feel like lead.
I'll try to switch my tassle,
    keep the board upon my head.
The cameras will be flashing,
    the clapping be a roar;
And we the class of '85
    will join those gone before.

But what have we accomplished?
    in spite of flowers and fuss?
If folks were really honest,
    would they be so proud of us?
Oh, we've got a lot of answers—
    in our knowledge we can bask;
But will our answers fit the questions
    the world is sure to ask?

There's a lot I haven't done—
    a lot I have neglected;
Many times I only did
    just what was then expected.
And then—what about the future,
    say ten years down the line?
Will Dad still be as proud
    and will my Mom's blue eyes still shine?

Will my toothless little brother
    grow up and point to me
And still claim me as his model
    What will the future be?
Oh, yes, I like the presents,
    the attention and acclaim;
But looking down the road ahead,
    will there be pride or shame?

Well, the band has struck the chord
    and the solemn march begins.
I'm glad it's called commencement,
    not the day a good thing ends.
Yes, I wonder what my future holds—
    the kind of man I'll be;
Well, here I go! I'm on my own—
    it all depends on me!

(Betty

Graduate's Prayer

Dear Lord, it was all so beautiful: marching down the aisle with my classmates all dressed up in our caps and gowns. The stirring speeches made me feel so grown up. Imagine—through with high school and on my own!

The picture-taking was fun even if I did get tired of posing. My hand aches from shaking so many hands—I'm glad some people hugged instead. The reception Mom put on for me was fantastic—all those little sandwiches! But I was too excited to eat. I can't believe Uncle George gave me fifty whole dollars! The other gifts were so nice, too, and the cards. They made me feel very special.

Now it's all over, and here I am, Lord, graduated. But that's not the end. It's really the beginning. Commencement, they said. Commencement of what? Further schooling? Which school? A job? Who would hire me? A life-mate after a while? I have so many questions, Lord.

I wouldn't admit this to anybody but You, Lord, but the big world seems awfully cold and a little bit scary. Will You help me to cope? Will You guide me to make the right decisions? Will You keep me from the bad things out there? Will You hold my hand when I start out on my own?

Thank You, Lord. It's not so scary now.

"With Thy counsel Thou wilt guide me, and afterward receive me to glory" (Psalm 73:24).

Moody Press, a ministry of the Moody Bible Institute, is designed for education, evangelization, and edification. If we may assist you in knowing more about Christ and the Christian life, please write us without obligation: Moody Press, c/o MLM, Chicago, Illinois 60610.